P9-AFO-698

Preservation Pantry

Modern Canning from Root to Top & Stem to Core

Preservation Pantry

SARAH MARSHALL

Regan Arts.

**Regan
Arts.**

New York, NY

The cooking techniques and methods presented in this book are the result of the author's experience. When cooking, care should be taken to use the proper materials and tools. The author and the publisher do not assume responsibility for any injury and/or damage to persons or property as a result of the use or misuse of the instructions and techniques contained in this book and are not liable for any damages or negative consequences from any action, application, or preparation, to any person reading or following the information in this book.

First Regan Arts edition,
September 2017

Library of Congress Control Number:
2017937177

ISBN 978-1-68245-006-2

Interior design by Alisha Petro

Cover design by Richard Ljoenes

Illustrations © Brooke Weeber

Food photography © Caleb Plowman

Food styling by Ashley Marti

Photograph of Tools and Equipment (page 16) © Rob Perry Photography; Stylist Kristin Lane

Photographs on pages v and xii by Molly Quan Photography

Printed in China

10 9 8 7 6 5 4 3 2 1

Dedication

To my best friend and husband, Dirk Marshall.

Thanks for the love, laughs, and being my biggest fan.

Contents

VEGETABLES: Root to Top

Introduction

My earliest memories are of gardening, cooking, and canning with my mom. She was born and raised in south San Francisco, but in 1975 she moved to Oregon to say good-bye to the city and live among the trees. Settling in Umpqua, she opened a small shop called Joy of Creations, where she sold handmade clothes and leather baby moccasins. She was a true entrepreneur. In every home we lived in, my mom grew a garden and made our food, canning lots of seasonal fruits and vegetables and using as much as she could from what the garden would yield. Next to my childhood desk sat a shelf that she lined with hundreds of jars of canned goods. She taught me how to can and, in return, I packed jars full of peaches, kept an eye on fermenting crocks of sauerkraut, and blended fruit for fruit leather. My mother instilled values in me of working hard together to feed our family, and she also passed on our family mantra: Food is love.

These values, rooted in nurturing and caring, set me on a family counseling career path. Over a decade ago, I finished school and started doing social work, and it was during this time that canning reentered my life. As I started a stressful case management job, the process of preserving the best part of something, from start to finish, became comforting. When I couldn't fix the problems or struggles of the people I wanted to heal, I fed them. My hope was that, for at least a few minutes, they knew someone was thinking about them. I also started canning jams and jellies for my parent groups, which eventually led me to teach those families how to can their own food. I made salsa and hot sauce bars for staff meetings and stayed up late baking pies with the fruit I had canned for our clinical reviews.

Due to budget cuts, I was in charge of running the at-risk youth programs as well as organizing the meals for those programs. My long work shifts were packed with crisis intervention, leaving no time to preserve the donated fruits and vegetables while on the job. Instead, I would come home from intense counseling sessions and can 50 pounds of donated tomatoes.

I canned everything, including jams, juices, jellies, and sauces—anything I was able to pick up at the food bank or gather produce from the program's on-site garden. After work, I really needed and looked forward to that quiet time in my kitchen. When I worked a retail job, I would dream about folding shirts. As a social worker, I would dream about trauma. When I started working with food I would dream about pickles and sauces—and finally my sleep was restful.

One lovely summer day, I was assigned to pick up a load of donated produce from the farmers' market. The farmers were excited that I could find a use for their end-of-the-day produce, and I would go back to tell them how much the kids in the program adored the applesauce that I had made from their apples. The clients especially liked the hot sauces I had started making. I became passionate and excited about developing recipes, and addicted to the joy it brought to the kids and families I made food for. I left the market that day with boxes full of berries and tomatoes, but I had found something more than just fresh produce—I had found my community and my passion.

Eventually, I decided to leave my job, which I did with a heavy heart, but my vision of the future was bright, with prospects of a new business and a new baby on the horizon. I registered for business classes and began developing recipes. In 2011, I started Marshall's Haute Sauce and was soon selling my hot sauces at the very same farmers' markets where I previously picked up produce. To this day, I buy all my produce from the farmers I first met, and work alongside my warmhearted farmer friends.

Every week at the farmers' market I have watched people gather to support one another, feed the community, and show gratitude for each other. Witnessing the hard work of the local farmers who grow delicious produce has given me a great appreciation for every part of a fruit and vegetable, especially the bits that are normally discarded or composted. We are aware that food waste is a huge national problem, and while much needs to change on an industrial level, not everyone knows that we can actually lessen the effects of food waste right in our very own kitchens.

I started using the root-to-top and stem-to-core methods while creating local small-batch hot sauces for my business. We use locally grown produce for all our products, and I noticed that far too much of this beautiful produce was going straight into the food waste bins. I started experimenting in the kitchen by drying pepper tops, boiling onion skins, and cooking down apple cores. Through much trial and error, I developed unique and delicious recipes that used parts of produce that most people would ordinarily just throw away. The recipes that follow highlight beautiful, sustainably grown produce, available at your local farmers' market, and honor the farmers who work hard to grow it.

Through simple, approachable steps, I will guide you through the process of canning seasonal fruits and vegetables, utilizing their normally discarded parts, and, finally, I will present recipes using these creations in delicious dishes. With these recipes I hope to offer you inspiration, from my own experience, to increase food preservation and decrease food waste.

There are so many simple things we can all do to help fight food waste. Notice and be mindful of your own food practices and try to be creative with leftover food scraps and items you might normally throw away; this will slowly start to become a natural routine for you and it's an easy first step to creating less waste. Give leftover produce to local organizations if you have a surplus of vegetables or a fruit tree. Donate your time by volunteering at your local food bank; the more volunteers there are, the quicker perishable food can get into the hands of those who need it. Organize canning clubs and food swaps (page 204); this helps us all to feel inspired to eat and preserve food in our communities. Or, create a community garden and donate the food. You can also share the recipes in this book with friends who have gardens, inspiring them to save produce.

I used to write service plans for the youth I worked with to encourage kids to do things differently than they had in the past. We would focus on what they could do better to promote positive change. I like to think of this book as a reflection of those plans. You don't need me to tell you there are problems with food waste and food production—that much is clear. What I can do is offer ideas and inspiration and encourage you to create a community that cares about food, healthy eating, and using all the beautiful produce around you. There are lots of people and organizations that inspire me because they make the fight against food waste a part of their daily lives. Find out about both national and local organizations that are helping to make a difference in the food community so you can see how you can contribute or help. (See Acknowledgments on page 216 for suggestions.)

In my past life as a social worker, I attempted to rescue those in crisis—families, individuals, and friends—who felt tossed aside and deemed unfit to shine. At times I was unsuccessful; clients and families continued to struggle with addiction and pain, and it broke my heart. However, in my food-focused community I have been successful at feeding people and bringing joy to their lives. It gives me hope and satisfaction and has been part of my own healing process.

At a time when the world can sometimes be dark and ugly, this cookbook is my way to bring people together and to encourage us to treasure each other and the food we eat. As individuals we should be cherished, and so should our food. This book is about cooking and canning in a full-use manner, but it is also about inspiring love and community through food.

Water Bath Canning Lesson

Water bath canning is a simple way to begin your canning experience, because you don't need any expensive equipment to get started. Though there are some simple rules, it really comes down to boiling water in a pot. If this is your first time canning, know that you can do this (pun intended), and after you run through it a few times, it may become an exciting, relaxing, and even meditative process.

1. locate a tested recipe

It may seem obvious, but the importance of this step cannot be overstated. Select recipes from a source that identifies proper temperature, headspace, and processing times; all need to be taken into account to safely can food at home. Trusted sources for canning recipes should follow the United States Department of Agriculture (USDA) and National Center for Home Food Preservation (NCFHFP) guidelines for safe practices. The recipes in this book have all been safety-tested at the Food Innovation Center in Portland, Oregon.

What is the risk of winging it? The biggest reason people are often wary of home preserving is the potential for botulism. Botulism is a rare type of food poisoning caused by the bacteria Clostridium botulinum. This toxin thrives in low-acid, room-temperature environments. I know kitchen science isn't for everyone, but for safety's sake, let me sum up the importance of pH in canning: If the pH of your sauce or preserve is low (below 3.9), then it is acidic. If the pH is high (above 4.0), then it is a low-acid product and it is not safe to water bath can. Adding an acid, such as vinegar, citrus, or citric acid, can lower the pH. The bacterium that causes botulism cannot thrive in an environment with a pH below 4.6.

The canning recipes in this book are either naturally acidic or acidified, meaning an acid (vinegar or citrus) is added to them during the cooking process, which makes them safe to water bath can. I personally test the pH of every batch of sauce or jam I make before canning, and I encourage you to do the same, because the pH of fresh ingredients can vary from plant to plant and fruit to fruit. Investing in a pH reader is a smart and affordable solution, if nothing else, for peace of mind. See Stocking Your Pantry, page 212 for my preferred pH reader.

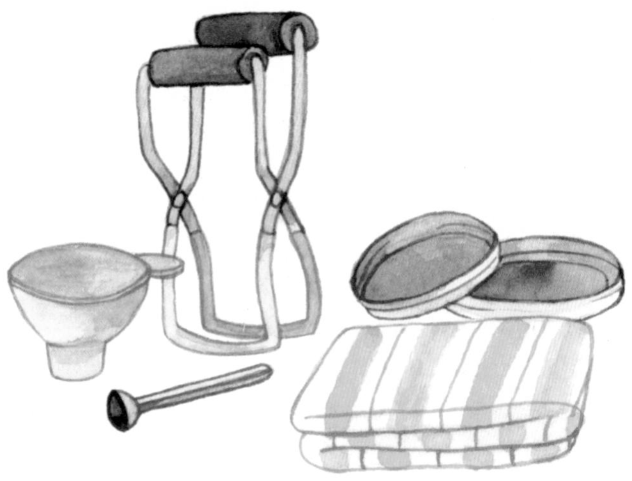

2. create a tidy filling station

People often come to my canning classes with stories of previous attempts to can at home, where they felt overwhelmed by the chaos it brought to their kitchens. Preparation and organization are critical to the canning process, and setting up stations will help keep you from feeling out of control. If you have ever visited a chef's kitchen or sat at a chef's counter, you may have noticed that each person involved in meal preparation has a well-organized station where food preparation, cooking, and plating take place. Meticulous prep keeps the space neat, minimizing dinner-rush mayhem. You don't need a restaurant-sized kitchen to channel that in your home; instead, you can stay in control by starting with efficient stations. My home kitchen is extremely small and my rolling cutting block takes a turn at each station.

Your at-home filling station should have everything you need for the bottling process, including:

Tea towel with two corners soaked in distilled vinegar

Kitchen towel to place hot jars on

Funnel

Heat-resistant pitcher

Ladle

Jar lifter

Chopstick, or another tool for removing air pockets

Magnetic lid lifter

Clean, new lids for jars

Metal bands for jars

---

3. clean the jars and lids

There are numerous brands and styles of jars on the market, but mason jars are the cheapest and easiest to locate. I recommend using jars paired with two-piece lids that have a safety button to indicate that the jars have sealed properly. For each recipe, I have given a jar size; while you may find that you have a larger or smaller jar on hand, I would advise sticking to the size I have suggested. Keep in mind that if you choose to use a larger jar, you will need to increase the processing time to ensure that the center of the contents get hot and the heat penetrates all the way through the contents of the jar.

I am often asked in classes if wide-mouth or small-mouth jars are preferred and my answer is: It depends on what you are canning. If you're packing large items, like pickles or sauerkraut, wide mouth is the way to go. The small-mouth jars are great for holding floating pickled items under the brine.

Washing your jars and lids is an important part of the canning

CANNING JAR SIZE CHART

quarter pint
(4 ounces)

half pint
small mouth
(8 ounces)

half pint
wide mouth
(8 ounces)

pint
wide mouth
(16 ounces)

quart
small mouth
(32 ounces)

quart
wide mouth
(32 ounces)

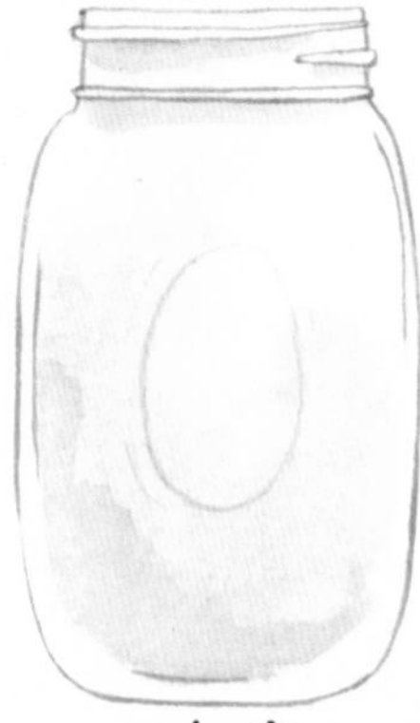

pint
small mouth
(16 ounces)

process. Especially if the jars are new, wash them with soap and water. New jars often have a rubber smell that a good bath easily takes care of. You can use a dishwasher, but washing by hand gives you the opportunity to inspect each jar. As you clean the jars, look for chips or cracks in the glass.

Always use new lids when canning because reused lids do not seal reliably. If you are using a standard two-piece lid, you can reuse the bands indefinitely, as long as they are clean and in good shape. According to the USDA Complete Guide to Home Canning, it is no longer necessary to boil lids in a separate pot, as they are sterilized during the water bath; instead, wash them and place them at your filling station in a clean bowl and pour 1 cup of boiling-hot water from the canning pot over them. Then use the magnetic lid lifter to safely take them out of the water.

I generally can in small batches. Processing smaller amounts of produce in a timely manner results in longer-lasting, better-quality canned goods. The recipes on the following pages will yield four to eight small jars. You can double or triple the recipe if you have a large amount of produce you want to preserve, but I do not recommend this route for jams, jellies, and preserves because it can affect the set of the preserves. Increasing batch sizes will also require increased cooking times and processing times. Remember, all produce is not created equal, and your recipes may result in one less or one more jar, be prepared by having an extra jar set on hand.

4. set up a stove station

The stove station is where the real magic happens. Preservation via water bath canning works in three phases. First, cooking these high-acid recipes keeps microorganisms from growing. Second, the boiling-water bath heats the food-filled jars, destroying more potential spoilers. Finally, a hermetic (airtight) seal is created, keeping that carefully built, bacteria-free environment stable. Although not really magic, it does feel magical when you hear the "popping" of a sealing jar.

This station should be equipped with everything necessary for heating and processing the jars, including:

One large canning pot with a lid

Rack that fits inside the canning pot

Clean jars that fit inside the pot

Water to cover the jars

Pots and pans for cooking

Your canning pot should be fitted with a rack to keep the jars from touching the bottom of the pot. Not using a rack is the most common way jars break. The whole bottom breaks off in one piece, and the contents are lost in an easily avoidable tragedy. I find the store-bought racks to be a bit rickety if I'm using various-sized jars. Instead, I recommend reinforcing the rack with a metal pizza screen, found at restaurant supply stores (see the Stocking Your Pantry section, page 212).

Place the rack in the bottom of the canning pot. Arrange the lidless jars in the pot, fill with water to cover the tops of the jars by 2 inches, 1 inch will be taken out later to heat the lids. On high heat, bring the covered pot to a boil. Turn heat to a low simmer, keeping the jars warm while you complete the next steps.

These recipes call for nonreactive pots and pans, meaning they will not break down when they come in contact with acid. I recommend stainless steel. Enamel and cast iron can both be affected from acidic ingredients and can either discolor your jams or ruin your pans. A proper stove station needs good pots, called saucepans here. Saucepans are tall and wide and generally fitted with a lid. Pans, on the other hand, are called skillets here. See Stocking Your Pantry section, page 212.

Key to size reference of pots and pans:

1–3 quarts	**small saucepan**
4–5 quarts	**medium saucepan**
6–7 quarts	**large saucepan**
8 quarts	**stockpot**
8-inch	**small skillet**
10-inch	**medium skillet**
12-inch	**large skillet**
Dutch oven	**large heat-resistant vessel with fitted lid**

When in the kitchen, I like to take things slow, whether I'm simmering, braising, or roasting. Good pans are very important for reducing sauces and infusing brines. The long process may seem like a waste of time when you read through the recipe, but once you taste the results, you will understand why these steps are listed. I usually make two to three of these recipes at a time, so if I picked up 100 pounds of tomatoes from the market, I am most likely roasting some in the oven, reducing sauce on the stove, and laying out the skins to be dried when the roasting is done. Slow down and enjoy your time at the stove station.

5. create a food preparation station

This station is where all the ingredients will be prepped and/or thoroughly washed and chopped, according to the recipe. Now is your chance to be sure that your ingredients are in great shape. Always compost produce with mold, spots, or browning. Canning is not like making banana bread; it is not a way to get rid of produce that has seen better days. Instead, canning preserves produce at its best.

Let's also talk about organic versus nonorganic produce. As these recipes call for skins, peels, and leaves, it is essential that you use produce grown using organic practices; in other words, produce that is not treated with chemicals. Many farms cannot afford organic certification; however, if you ask farmers directly, they will tell you if they use chemical sprays or pesticides. The chance to have these important conversations is a great reason to shop at your local farmers' market. For instance, some berry farmers will spray before the berries produce fruit, so you would not want to use those for the Strawberry Top Salad Dressing (page 115), because these plants have been directly exposed to chemical sprays.

The preparation station is where some of the behind-the-scenes work takes place. Taking time with your cuts will elevate your canning game. Good knife skills can transform vegetables into visually stunning pickles. My husband, Dirk, is the master of our prep station. He takes the time to make sure each carrot coin is exactly ¼ inch, each beet cube is perfectly square, and every seed is removed from his expertly halved kumquats. This is, of course, above and beyond and not a necessary skill to make pickles, but the more you practice, the better you will get.

CHOPPING CHART

Chop

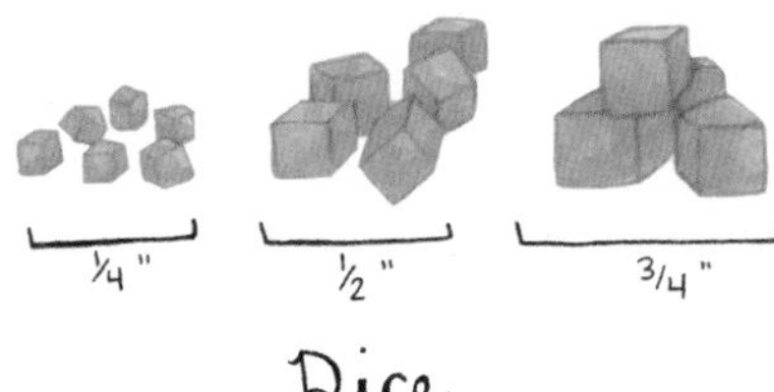

Dice

Mince

Brunoise or Finely Mince

Julienne or Matchsticks

Chiffonade

Coins

Slice Whole

Your perfect preparation station should consist of:

Colander

Washcloth for scrubbing skins of root vegetables

Large cutting board

Kitchen towel beneath cutting board

Large, sharp chef's knife and small paring knife

Optional (but highly recommended) preparation equipment:

Blender

Food processor

Immersion blender

After the produce is washed, chopped, and measured, portion out all other ingredients. Dirk likes to put the ingredients in separate bowls and cups for easy access during the cooking process. When he does this for me, I feel like kitchen royalty, with everything I could want at my fingertips. Treat yourself by organizing your ingredients this way. There is a French term for this style of setup called *mise en place*, meaning "everything in its place." I suggest reading the recipe and then premeasuring all the ingredients to have them on hand and already prepared when you start cooking.

This cookbook includes quite a few sauce recipes, as these are my specialty. Making a nicely textured sauce requires specific tools, one being an immersion blender. Although you can use a standing blender, it gets a bit messy, doesn't blend as well, and you run the risk of getting burned when handling the hot sauces. You can purchase an immersion blender at most kitchen stores; look for one with a stainless steel stick. There are some that have a plastic stick; these can melt at higher temperatures. See Stocking Your Pantry section, page 212.

You can get away with just the immersion blender, but if you want to get a smooth texture with no skins or seeds, you will also need a high-quality blender, see Stocking Your Pantry section, page 212. No matter how long you use your mortar and pestle, an onion skin will not become a powder unless you use a blender that has an airflow fan inside. If you do not have one that will grind the skins and seeds, you can use a food mill or cheesecloth, but this will change the texture of the sauces and especially change the cooking times.

6. make the jam, sauce, or pickles

Follow the recipe using exact measured amounts. Once the recipe is complete, I use my pH reader to make sure it is well below 4.1 before filling the jars. If your pH is reading above 4.0, there may have been an error in the ratio of produce to acid or the fruit may have been more ripe, resulting in a higher pH, so add a splash of vinegar or citrus, heat for a few minutes, and test it again.

There are ways that you can safely make these recipes your own. If you would like to substitute one kind of vinegar for another, feel free to do so—but pay attention to the acidity level. Distilled vinegar has an acidity of 5 percent, so choose a vinegar that has at least the same level of acidity. I have selected the vinegar in these recipes based on a balance of flavors. If I am working with sweet ingredients, I tend to pair them with a balancing vinegar, like rice or distilled. If I want the result to be sweeter, I use vinegars of the fruit variety, like white balsamic, white wine, or champagne. I find these to be mellow in flavor, with a hint of fruit that balances the spicy heat well.

You can also switch out spices. For instance, if you are making the Carrot Cumin Slaw (page 135) and you are not a fan of cumin seeds, replace the cumin with 1 tablespoon of toasted sesame seeds. This will not affect the pH in a significant way if you are using the same measured amount called for in the recipe.

7. fill the jars to recommended headspace

To keep everything hot, fill one jar at a time. Pull the jar out of the canner using a jar lifter and pour the water out of the jar back into the canning pot. Set the jar onto your filling station and place a funnel into the jar. To transport the brine, sauce, or jam from the pot to the jar, I recommend using a 2-quart, heat-resistant pitcher. It gives more control when pouring. You can also use a ladle, but that can be a bit messy.

Headspace is a measured amount of open space from the top of the jar to the contents in the jar. Canning recipes typically call for ¼ inch of headspace for jams and sauces, ½ inch of headspace for pickles, or 1 inch for anything that might expand during the water bath process. Overfilling the headspace is where some sealing issues occur, so make sure to follow the suggested fill measurements.

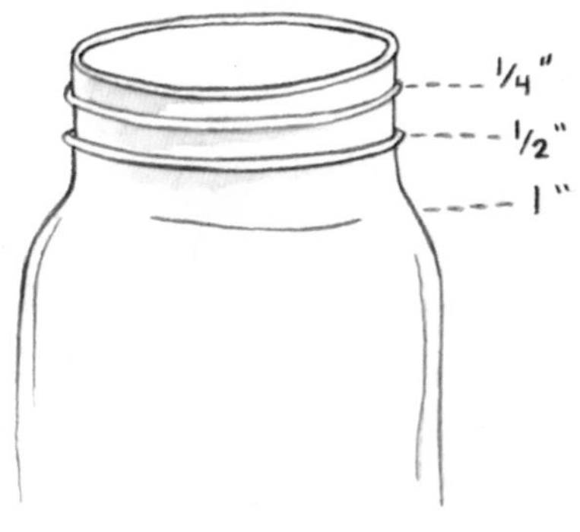

Too little headspace can cause overflow, cracked jars, or warped lids—all resulting in seal failure. If you overfill jars, simply use a measuring spoon to remove jam or brine before screwing on the lids. Too much headspace can cause cracks in jars, discoloration, and require a longer processing time. If the jar is not filled to at least 1 inch from the top, either move it to a smaller jar or set it aside to refrigerate and eat later.

On rare occasions a jar will break during the canning process, and this is most likely to happen at your stove station. Broken jars are part of working with glass, but the inevitability doesn't make it any less heartbreaking. Jars most often break due to temperature issues, but there are many other causes. Keeping both jars and filling contents hot helps decrease the likelihood of a broken jar. The water in the water bath pot doesn't need to be bubbling away, but a low simmer is ideal.

8. remove the air pockets, wipe the rim, secure the lid

Your filling station contains all the tools necessary for ensuring a good seal. Air pockets or bubbles can get trapped in the jars, especially in pickles and thick sauces. If bubbles are not removed, the contents may appear to be carbonated. Removing these air bubbles also helps create an accurate headspace measurement. To get rid of the air pockets, run a chopstick or a small rubber spatula along the inside of the jar, or gently tap the jars on a kitchen towel. If you notice that there is a significant drop in the headspace, add a bit more brine. Next, wipe the rim of the jar with the corner of the vinegar-soaked tea towel. This process helps to make certain that there are no particles or sticky matter that will get between the glass rim and the plastic seal of the lid. Then place the new, clean lid on the jar. Hold the lid in place on the rim of the jar, set the band, and tighten ("finger tight," not with the full torque of your arm).

9. place jars in the canner

Using the jar lifter, gently place the jars in the water bath, lowering them onto the canning rack. Jars should be covered by 1 inch of water, so add hot tap water to the canning pot if you are short. Adding cold water to the pot may crack the jars. Place the lid on the canning pot.

10. bring to a boil, start processing time, remove lid, and let sit for 5 minutes

Bring the canner to a boil on high heat. Start the required processing time once the water is at a full rolling boil, which means it has reached 212°F. If needed, adjust the processing time based on your elevation.

After the canner has boiled for the required time, turn off the heat on the stove and remove the lid of the canning pot. Let the jars sit in the pot for 5 minutes more. If you look in the pot, you will see air bubbles escaping from the jars. This released air helps to create a proper seal. Oxygen escapes from the jars during the boiling process, and when the contents cool later, the lids will seal because of suction.

ELEVATION CHART

These recipes are written for altitudes below 1,000 feet.

Boiling water point goes ↓ as altitude goes ↑

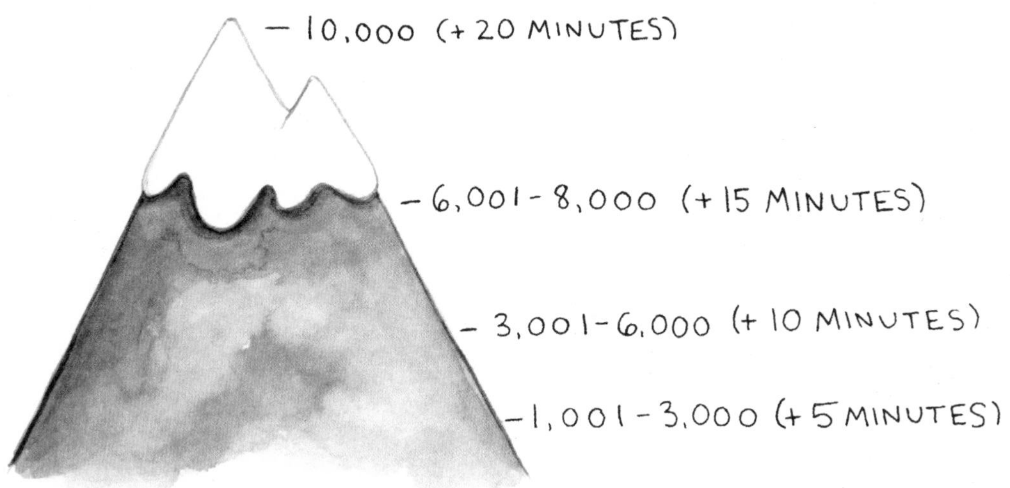

11. remove jars and place on a towel, let stand 24 hours

Gently remove the jars from the canning pot with either a jar lifter or a lifting rack. Pull the jars straight up without tipping or turning them, as this might break the seal or cause the jars to tip and break. Place them on a tea towel or a cutting board, as they will be very hot. Let them sit for 24 hours. You may hear them pop or seal, but just let them be.

12. check seals and label jars

Four hours after taking the jars out of the pot, check to see that the jars have sealed. You can do this by pushing on the lid; if it gives, the jar has not sealed. It is still safe to eat, but it is not shelf-stable and should be kept in the refrigerator.

Label each jar with the contents and expiration date, one year from the processing date. Keep the labels simple, small, and clean. Cut out a circle the size of the lid top on heavy cardstock, remove the band, place the label on top of the jar, and replace the band to hold the label in place.

Store your filled canning jars in a dark, cool place, such as a cabinet or the cellar. This helps to keep the jars sealed and also retain the desired color. Although it doesn't happen frequently, dispose of any jars if the lids are bulging, unsealed, moldy on top, or hissing.

2
1
13
11
10
15
16
3
14
19
12
5
18
20
4
9
24
Vitamix
43
7
6
48
40
23
22
8
31
36
21
27
29
50
34
KitchenAid
42
45
44
49
37
46
33
KitchenAid
39
25
47
41
32
30
28
35
38
26
17

Fundamental Tools and Equipment

I have always lived in small houses with very little storage space. My canning pot has a permanent spot on top of our kitchen cabinets and is filled with all my canning supplies. While you don't need all these special gadgets and tools, there are some items called for in the recipes that are very helpful to have on hand.

TOOLS FOR THE FOOD PREPARATION STATION

1 Colander
2 Cutting board
3 Kitchen towel
4 Paring knife
5 Sharp chef's knife

OPTIONAL EQUIPMENT FOR THE FOOD PREPARATION STATION

6 Blender
7 Food processor
8 Immersion blender

TOOLS FOR THE FILLING STATION

9 Canning jars
10 Chopstick (air-pocket remover)
11 Heat-resistant pitcher
12 Jar lifter
13 Ladle
14 Lids and bands
15 Magnetic lid lifter
16 pH reader
17 Small-mouth funnel
18 Thermometer
19 Wide-mouth funnel

TOOLS FOR THE STOVE STATION

20 Canning pot with lid
21 Jam pot
22 Pots (saucepans)
23 Pans (skillets)
24 Rack that fits into canning pot

OTHER HELPFUL KITCHEN ESSENTIALS

25 Baking mat (silicon)
26 Baking sheet
27 Cheesecloth
28 Citrus juicer
29 Fine-mesh strainer
30 Ice cream scoop
31 Jelly bag
32 Kitchen scale
33 Kitchen timer
34 Measuring spoons
35 Measuring cups
36 Microplane
37 Mixing bowls
38 Pastry brush
39 Potato masher
40 Rolling pin
41 Slotted spoon
42 Stand mixer
43 Tongs
44 Vegetable peeler
45 Wire whisk

TOOLS FOR BASIC PRESERVING

46 Fermentation mason jar cap
47 Fermentation mason jar weight
48 Mortar and pestle
49 Salt block
50 Spice grinder

Fruits: Stem to Core

apples

Often forgotten as a seasonal fruit, apples are most delightful when plucked right off the tree in the middle of autumn. Orchard season kicks off fall in the Pacific Northwest, and as soon as the first apples arrive at the market, we know summer has come to an end and apple season is just beginning. From the sweet Honeycrisp to the beautiful Pink Lady to the tart Jonagold, all varieties are special in their own way. I first learned about apple varieties while searching for the perfect apple for our Ghost Chili Sauce. I wanted a high-sugar-content apple, one that would not darken quickly and would balance the spice of the hot peppers. My research included a day spent tasting apples in an orchard in Hood River to find the perfect one. Hunting for that specific taste led me to understand different varieties and how they can best be showcased, highlighting the fruit and putting a piece of fall onto the pantry shelf. The skins of apples are full of vitamin C and dietary fiber, and the following recipes incorporate the often-cast-aside peels.

Canned

GINGER LIQUEUR SPIKED APPLES

This recipe has become a fall ritual in our home and I think it tastes even better if you pick the apples yourself. From canning club to family dinner, I keep jars of these on hand to make sweet treats for every gathering I host. Use these apples to fill pies, tarts, muffins, and crumbles. Ginger liqueur is often made in France with cognac and can be found at most liquor stores (see Stocking Your Pantry, page 212), or you can even make your own by soaking fresh ginger in cognac.

6 pounds Honeycrisp apples, divided

¼ cup fresh lemon juice (from 2 large lemons), divided

1 cup light brown sugar, lightly packed

1 tablespoon ground cinnamon

1 teaspoon ground nutmeg

¼ teaspoon ground star anise

7 tablespoons ginger liqueur, divided

Makes 6 pints

Assemble the canning stations as described on pages 5–7, steps 2–4. At the preparation station, wash the apples under cold running water. Set 2 apples aside for later. Place 4 cups of cold water into a bowl and add 2 tablespoons of lemon juice and stir. Using a sharp paring knife, cut the core out of the apples by slicing each side off around the core, leaving a square core. Cut the apples into ¼-inch cubes, leaving the peels on. Place the cubed apples into the bowl of lemon water.

Skin and core the remaining 2 apples, cut into medium-size slices, and save the cores and peels for the Whiskey Apple-Core Caramel recipe on page 24. Put the sliced apples into a food processor, add the remaining lemon juice, and blend until smooth, about 2 minutes.

In a large saucepan, place 2 cups of water, the brown sugar, and apple mixture from the food processor, all the spices, and 1 tablespoon of ginger liqueur. Bring to a boil over high heat, about 3 minutes. Once it boils, give the pot a stir and turn the heat to low. Let simmer uncovered.

After 15 minutes of simmering, drain the soaking apple cubes in a colander in the sink. Add the apple cubes to the pot and stir gently. Cook for 5 minutes over medium heat, stir again, and cook for another 5 minutes. Turn the heat to the lowest setting.

At the filling station, keep the jars and apples hot while filling each jar. Place 1 tablespoon of ginger liqueur into each jar. Use a funnel and ladle to place the apples into the jar, leaving 1 inch of headspace. Use a heat-resistant pitcher to top the jar off with syrup from the pot, leaving ½ inch of headspace. Remove the air pockets, wipe the rim, and secure the lid. Place the jars in the water bath, covered by 1 inch of water. Once the water is boiling, process for 20 minutes (pages 11–14, steps 7–12).

TIP

You can use this same recipe to make homemade applesauce. Simply peel all the apples and cook them for 30 minutes, rather than 5, then run them through the food processor. It's up to you to leave in or take out the liqueur.

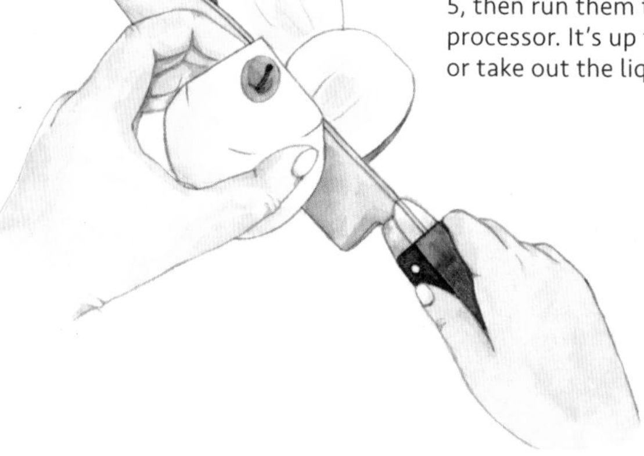

Remove the peel with a sharp pairing knife, cut the core into a square by slicing each side of the apple.

TIP

You can use these apples to make the Drunken Apple Crumble (page 27).

TIP
This applesauce makes a lovely gift, especially paired with the recipe card for Matcha Tea Applesauce Breakfast Bowl on page 23.

Canned

MATCHA TEA APPLESAUCE

Matcha is a green tea powder made from young, shade-grown tea leaves and is packed with antioxidants and amino acids. Depending on the variety, it can be very earthy or deeply rich. We are lucky to have an artisan producer here in Portland called Mizuba. Their version is mild with a hint of vanilla. I always need to grab a quick breakfast before running off to the market and this is the perfect power breakfast to get me ready for my day.

6 Granny Smith apples

¼ cup fresh lemon juice (from 2 large lemons)

1 teaspoon matcha tea powder

1 cup boiling water

2-inch piece of ginger, peeled and finely grated

1 tablespoon local honey

½ teaspoon ground cinnamon

Makes 6 half-pints

Assemble the canning stations as described on pages 5–7, steps 2–4. At the food preparation station, wash the apples under cold running water. Cut out the cores of the apples and save for the Whiskey Apple-Core Caramel recipe on page 24. Chop the apples into large chunks and place them in a bowl. Pour the lemon juice over the apples.

Place the matcha tea powder in a glass vessel and add the hot water slowly, stirring with a spoon, until it's dissolved and there are no visible clumps.

Place the apples with the lemon juice, the dissolved matcha, ginger, honey, and cinnamon in a medium, nonreactive pot. Cover and simmer over medium heat for 20 minutes, stirring occasionally. Turn the heat to the lowest setting and blend with an immersion blender until smooth.

At the filling station, keep the jars and applesauce hot while packing each jar. Pour the sauce into a heat-resistant pitcher. Use a funnel and fill each jar, leaving ½ inch of headspace. Remove the air pockets, wipe the rim, and secure the lid. Place jars in the water bath, covered by 1 inch of water. Once the water is boiling, process for 10 minutes (page 11–14, steps 7–12).

Recipe

Makes 1 breakfast bowl

title: MATCHA TEA APPLESAUCE BREAKFAST BOWL

directions:

1 half-pint Matcha Tea Applesauce, ¼ cup fresh blueberries, ¼ cup fresh raspberries, 2 tablespoons sliced almonds, 1 tablespoon shredded coconut

Place the Matcha Tea Applesauce in a bowl. Garnish with blueberries, raspberries, sliced almonds, and shredded coconut.

Preserved

WHISKEY APPLE-CORE CARAMEL

I often use booze in my recipes. When my canning club, the Portland Preservation Society, first started, we created a contest to see whose canned goods everyone liked best (see page 204). The first person who had all his or her canned goods chosen would get a prize, and I often won. My secret? I realized people loved canned goods even more if you added a dash of alcohol. I have made just about everything with a little booze, and this recipe happens to be one of my favorites. The touch of apple from the rescued skins and cores gives a new depth to this luscious caramel sauce.

¼ cup, plus 2 tablespoons whiskey, divided

6 apple cores, stems and seeds included (reserved from Ginger Liqueur Spiked Apples, page 20)

1 cinnamon stick

1 cup granulated sugar

6 tablespoons salted butter

½ cup heavy whipping cream

Makes 4 quarter-pints

TIP
Use this caramel to make the Drunken Apple Crumble (page 27). →

Place ¼ cup of whiskey, apple cores, and cinnamon stick into a small saucepan. Heat on medium-high heat for 10 minutes, then turn down to low heat and simmer for 20 minutes. Stir the mixture as it's simmering and look for all the liquid to cook out of the pan and into the apples.

Once the liquid has cooked out and the apples are soft, remove the cinnamon stick, place the contents into a food processor, and pulse until smooth. Pour the contents from the food processor into a jelly bag or double-layered cheesecloth. Squeeze the liquid through the bag and into a measuring cup. It will take some strong squeezing to get the tasty liquid and pulp through the jelly bag.

In a large, heavy-bottom, stainless steel pot, place ¼ cup of the strained apple liquid, sugar, and the remaining 2 tablespoons of whiskey. Heat on medium-high heat, swirling the pan gently. Move the pan in a circular motion over the heat. Do not stir; simply swirl the pan every 2 minutes, for about 10 to 15 minutes.

When the liquid is a deep amber color, reduce the heat to medium-low. Add the butter and cream. The contents in the pot will bubble and boil up a bit. When it dies down, swirl it gently. Continue swirling and heating for 5 to 10 minutes, or until the contents are a deep caramel color.

Remove the caramel from the heat and pour into jars. Let it cool before putting lids on. Caramel can be stored in the refrigerator for up to 3 months.

TIPS
If you do not have apple scraps to make the apple core mixture, simply substitute ¼ cup of apple juice instead.

Just put the spoon away. Better yet, don't even pull it out of the drawer. You don't need it. Using a spoon may cause crystallization and a grainy caramel. Instead, swirl, swirl, swirl!

Recipe

DRUNKEN APPLE CRUMBLE

My grandmother always made crisps and crumbles. They are a quick and easy way to make a fast dessert, highlighting fruit. The butter, flour, sugar, and spices needed for this recipe are part of a well-stocked pantry. You can play around with spices, nuts, and oats, but this recipe keeps it simple, so as not to distract from the delicious apples. This combo is extra thick and gooey, resulting in a comforting dessert and the perfect vehicle for ice cream. Make this crisp in a Dutch oven over a campfire and enjoy under the stars.

½ cup unsalted butter

1 cup all-purpose flour

½ cup light brown sugar

½ teaspoon ground cinnamon

¼ teaspoon ground nutmeg

¼ teaspoon kosher salt

2 pints Ginger Liqueur Spiked Apples (page 20)

1 quarter-pint jar Whiskey Apple-Core Caramel (page 24)

Makes 1 crumble

Preheat the oven to 350°F.

Melt the butter in a medium saucepan over medium heat. Set aside.

In a medium bowl, mix the flour, brown sugar, cinnamon, nutmeg, and salt. Drizzle in the melted butter and stir to combine.

Open 2 pint jars of Ginger Liqueur Spiked Apples and place them into a greased pie pan. Crumble the mixture on top of the apples, creating a ½-inch crust.

Place the pie pan on a rimmed baking sheet. Bake for 25–30 minutes, until golden. Remove the crumble from the oven and drizzle the Whiskey Apple-Core Caramel on top. Serve immediately.

TIP

If you did not can the Ginger Liqueur Spiked Apples, you can still make this crisp by substituting with canned apples or berries.

Cherries

Cherries in Oregon are mostly grown in orchards along the shadowed valleys of Mt. Hood. These farms hold a special place in my heart because I grew up here. The stone fruit orchards have a small window to harvest the Royal Ann's, pie cherries, and tart cherries we are best known for. With an extremely short picking season—just one month—we take full advantage of putting up cherries. They are the first fruit trees to produce at the end of summer, and the yearly Hood River Cherry Festival always celebrates their arrival. Cherries have a fantastic depth of flavor; they are wonderful fresh, but the sweetness really deepens with drying and curing. While the cherry fruit contains a natural melatonin that can promote healthy sleep, the cherry stone also contains healthy molecules that promote strong bone and muscle health. It's not a good idea to eat the cherry stones (they contain trace amounts of cyanide), but this chapter will show you how to use the stones to extract those healthy molecules within.

Canned

BOURBON BRINED CHERRIES

These cherries are perfect for your next cocktail, fruit salad, or even a late-night snack. A hearty dose of bourbon and a mix of warming spices give the brine a lovely depth of flavor, while the vinegar adds an enticing zing, and it's all finished with a delicate almond note. These cherries will go quickly and, after they do, save the brine for salad dressings, cocktails, and drizzling on frozen yogurt.

2 pounds cherries, stems removed

2 cups apple cider vinegar

2 cups bourbon

1 cup light brown sugar, lightly packed

1 cinnamon stick

5 whole cloves

5 whole peppercorns

1 tablespoon almond extract

Makes 6 half-pints

Assemble the canning stations as described on pages 5–7, steps 2–4. At the food preparation station, wash the cherries under cold running water and compost or eat any soft or blemished fruit. Remove the stones with a cherry pitter or knife and save them for the Cherry Stone Bitters recipe (page 31).

In a large saucepan, place the apple cider vinegar, bourbon, brown sugar, cinnamon stick, cloves, peppercorns, and almond extract. Bring to a boil over high heat. Once boiling, turn the heat to low and let simmer for 10 minutes.

At the filling station, pack the cherries into the hot jars, leaving 1 inch of headspace. Use a funnel and a heat-resistant pitcher to cover them with syrup, leaving ½-inch headspace. Tap the jar lightly on a kitchen towel to remove air bubbles trapped in the pitted cherries. Add brine if necessary, wipe the rim, and secure the lid. Place the jars in the water bath, covered by 1 inch of water. Once the water is boiling, process for 10 minutes (pags 11–14, steps 7–12).

TIPS

These cherries are delicious dropped into Manhattan cocktails. If you plan to use them for cocktails, leave the stems on the cherries.

After you have eaten the cherries, save the brine for the Kale and Apple Salad with Cherry Brine Dressing (page 32).

Canned

DRIED CHERRY MUSTARD

Our Portland Farmers Market stand is next to a lovely couple who own and operate a cherry farm just south of the city. Cherry season in Oregon is brief, so we are lucky to have them as neighbors; we never miss out on fresh cherries. To preserve what they can of their blink-and-you-miss-it fruit season, they dry a portion of their precious crop. This mustard has become a go-to recipe to make in the winter when I am craving their tart treats and it's a perfect addition to any turkey sandwich.

2¼ cups yellow mustard seeds

3 cups dried cherries

2 cups red wine vinegar

¾ cup mustard powder

3 tablespoons kosher salt

1 teaspoon black pepper, finely ground

Makes 6 pints

At the food preparation station, place the mustard seeds in a medium bowl, add 4 cups of cold water, and soak for 10 minutes. Mince the cherries. After soaking time is complete, drain the seeds through a fine-mesh strainer. In a large bowl, combine the mustard seeds, cherries, red wine vinegar, 3 cups of cold water, mustard powder, salt, and pepper, until well mixed. Cover the bowl with plastic wrap and refrigerate for 24 hours.

Assemble the canning stations as described on page 5–7, steps 2–4. In a medium saucepan, heat the mustard mixture over medium-low heat.

(CONTINUED)

(CONTINUED)

When the mustard is warm, begin blending with an immersion blender until well combined. (Note: There will still be whole mustard seeds.) After blending, reduce over medium-low heat for 5 to 10 minutes until desired consistency.

At the filling station, keep the jars and mustard hot while filling each jar. Use a funnel and spoon to fill each jar, leaving ½ inch of headspace. Remove the air pockets by pressing the mustard down and by tapping the jar gently on a kitchen towel. Wipe the rim and secure the lid. Place the jars in the water bath covered by 1 inch of water. Once the water is boiling, process for 10 minutes (page 11–14, steps 7–12).

TIP

You can substitute other dried fruit, such as apricots, cranberries, or apples, for the cherries.

Preserved

CHERRY STONE BITTERS

Time-consuming, messy, and above all, labor-intensive, pitting cherries has never been my favorite kitchen task. In fact, it is so notoriously laborious that pitted cherries were historically a treat for royalty. Knowing that I will get use out of the cherries as well as the stones gets me through the tedious job. Cherry Bitters like these are often used in cocktails, but they can also be used in salad dressings, especially of the fruit variety.

½ cup cherry stones (reserved from Bourbon Brined Cherries, page 29)

3 tablespoons dried lavender

1 tablespoon dried orange peel

1 tablespoon dried lemon peel

1 teaspoon coriander

½ teaspoon cherry bark

¼ teaspoon gentian root

¼ teaspoon fennel seeds

2 cardamom pods

1 star anise

¾ cup vodka

Makes 4 ounces

Place the cherry stones and the remaining dry ingredients in a 1-quart mason jar. Cover the ingredients with the vodka and a ½ cup of room-temperature water. Secure a screw-top lid. Place the jar into a dark cabinet and let cure for 15 days, shaking the jar occasionally.

After 15 days, strain the liquid through a fine-mesh strainer, then through a coffee filter to remove any fine particles, compost the remaining stones and pulp. Store in a cool dark cabinet for up to 1 year.

TIPS

This makes a great gift with a cocktail recipe attached. It is best to store these bitters in a small bottle fitted with a dropper or an orifice reducer.

Cherry bark and gentian root can be sourced from a spice and herb supplier (see Stocking Your Pantry on page 212).

Use this recipe to make the Party Punch (page 208).

CAUTION

When using roots and barks, use whole pieces, rather than powders, so they can be easily strained and not ingested. Follow the recipe and don't increase quantities. Use only a few drops of bitters at a time.

Recipe

KALE AND APPLE SALAD WITH CHERRY BRINE DRESSING

I grew up knowing that if we were going to dinner in the northwest neighborhood of Portland we were undoubtedly celebrating something: a birthday, a wedding, or an anniversary. Twenty years later, nothing has changed. I still celebrate special moments in one of a handful of restaurants in NW. At Serrato, one of our go-to celebration spots, Chef Tony Meyers makes an extra-special kale salad, and this is my tribute to that dish. Dinosaur kale, also called lacinato, is a type of kale that is quite tender and thus perfect for raw salads like this.

1 medium bunch dinosaur kale (about 4 cups, chopped)

1 medium Honeycrisp apple

2-inch rectangle Parmigiano-Reggiano cheese

3 tablespoons extra virgin olive oil

2 tablespoons apple cider vinegar

1 tablespoon brine from Bourbon Brined Cherries (page 29)

¼ cup pine nuts

10 Bourbon Brined Cherries (page 29)

Makes 4 servings

In a large bowl, place cold water with 3 ice cubes, and soak the kale for 10 minutes until cold and crisp. Drain the water and dry the kale on a kitchen towel.

Meanwhile, at the preparation station, wash and cut the apple into ½-inch cubes. Shred the Parmigiano-Reggiano on the finest box grater option. Whisk together the olive oil, apple cider vinegar, and Bourbon Brined Cherries brine to form an emulsified dressing. Set all aside.

In a small dry skillet, toast the pine nuts over medium heat. Shake the skillet every 15 seconds for about 3 minutes, until golden and fragrant, then quickly move the nuts to a plate to stop cooking.

Slice the kale along the stem on each side and finely mince the stem. Chiffonade the leaves of kale.

In a large bowl, toss the kale, apple cubes, toasted pine nuts, and dressing until evenly coated. Arrange on a platter and top with the Bourbon Brined Cherries and Parmigiano-Reggiano cheese.

TIP

If you did not make the Bourbon Brined Cherries, you can substitute with ¼ cup of dried cherries and 1 tablespoon of cherry juice for the brine.

Grapes

You can't think of Oregon without thinking of grapes—even our state flower is the Oregon grape. Most Oregonians have some personal experience with vineyards. We work on vineyards, go on wine tastings, and sometimes even get married in the groves. The places our grapes grow have a special significance, and the fruit does too. My husband and I make wine with grapes (Red Haute Pinot). Our local boutique caterers (Tournant) even cook seafood over burning grapevines at elaborate dinners. Ingrained in local traditions, grapes are held in high regard; we honor the vines, the leaves, and especially the fruit. This chapter encourages grape-skin consumption, which reduces food waste and promotes heart health at the same time. Grape skins contain resveratrol, which can act as a protectant against damage to the heart.

Tarragon Pickled Grapes, page 36.

Canned

TARRAGON PICKLED MUSCAT GRAPES

Muscat grapes are grown in Oregon, but can also be found in larger specialty stores around the country when they're in season. They are plump, perfectly round, and often have a slight pink hue. If you can't find this varietal, you can substitute any seedless grape. These pickled grapes, with their puckering punch, make a lovely, unexpected addition to a cheese board or salad. You can substitute other fresh herbs for the tarragon if you prefer, but I like the earthy, light note the herbs lend to the juicy-sweet grapes.

3 pounds Muscat grapes (about 8 cups)

½ cup fresh lemon juice, plus 12 round lemon slices (from about 4 large lemons, divided)

4 cups white balsamic vinegar

2 tablespoons kosher salt

1 tablespoon granulated sugar

7 sprigs fresh tarragon, divided

7 sprigs fresh thyme, divided

1½ teaspoons pink peppercorns, divided

Makes 6 pints

Assemble the canning stations as described on pags 5–7, steps 2–4. At the food preparation station, wash the grapes and remove the stems. Wash and slice 4 lemons into ¼-inch-thick rounds, a total of 12 rounds. Juice the remaining 2 lemons, reserving ½ cup juice.

In a medium saucepan, place the vinegar, 2 cups of water, ½ cup reserved lemon juice, salt, sugar, 1 sprig tarragon, and 1 sprig thyme. Bring to a boil over high heat. Once boiling, turn the heat to a low simmer and let the mixture infuse for 10 minutes. Remove the tarragon and thyme with tongs, and compost.

At the filling station, keep the jars and brine hot while filling each jar. Place ¼ teaspoon of pink peppercorns into the bottom of each jar. Pack cold grapes into the jar, filling halfway. Place one lemon slice against one wall in each jar to ensure visibility. Add the remaining herb sprigs to the opposite side. Fill with the grapes, leaving 1 inch of headspace. Top the jars with the brine, leaving 1 inch of headspace, lay a slice of lemon on top and cover with brine, leaving ¾ inch of headspace. Remove the air pockets, wipe the rim, and secure the lid. Place the jars in the water bath, covered by 1 inch of water. Once the water is boiling, process for 10 minutes (page 11–14, steps 7–12).

TIPS

I have tried this recipe with just about every herb. Thyme flowers and their purple hue are my second herb choice because they make for a lovely display.

Please note that the grapes will expand, so leave that extra recommended headspace so your jars don't overflow.

Use the Tarragon Pickled Grapes to make the Blue Cheese and Grape Brioche Flatbread (page 40).

Canned

GRAPE JAM WITH TOASTED PINE NUTS

I started making this for my daughter for our picnic lunches. Peanut butter and jelly is not difficult to make, but this recipe is even easier and is a fun twist on an old favorite. The pine nuts take the place of the traditional peanut butter, adding protein and a nice crunch. This jam is also a great addition to cheese plates. If you want to make an extra-special lunch for a tiny gal—as I often do—this is the way to do it.

2 pounds red seedless grapes

2 pounds white seedless grapes

½ cup fresh lemon juice, plus lemon peels (from about 2 large lemons)

½ cup pine nuts

3 cups granulated sugar

Makes 5 half-pints

Assemble the canning stations as described on page 5–7, steps 2–4. At the preparation station, wash all the grapes under cold running water and remove the stems from the fruit. Using a paring knife, cut off the lemon peels and slice them into large strips. Cut the lemons in half and juice, setting aside ½ cup juice.

In a small, dry skillet, toast the pine nuts over medium heat. Shake the skillet every 15 seconds for about 3 minutes, until they're golden and fragrant, then quickly move the nuts to a plate to stop cooking. Set aside.

Place the grapes in a large heavy-bottom skillet. Over medium heat, warm the grapes while gently smashing them with the back of a wooden spoon to release their juices. Add the sugar, lemon peels, and the lemon juice to the pan. Bring to a boil over high heat, stirring frequently to avoid burning. Once bubbling, turn the heat to a low simmer and cook for 45 minutes to 1 hour, stirring often. When the jam is thick enough to coat the back of a spoon, turn off the heat and stir in the pine nuts. Remove the lemon peels with tongs and compost them. Let the jam sit for 5 minutes to set; this will keep the pine nuts from floating to the top.

At the filling station, keep the jars and jam hot while filling each jar. Use a large spoon and a funnel to fill the jars with jam, leaving ¼ inch of headspace. Remove the air pockets, wipe the rim, and secure the lid. Place the jars in the water bath, covered by 1 inch of water. Once the water is boiling, process for 10 minutes (pages 11–14, steps 7–12).

TIP

If grape skins bother you or your little one, you can strain the skins through a jelly bag overnight and stir in the pine nuts after straining.

Canned

PICKLED GRAPE LEAVES

I like having these on hand for an impromptu appetizer or snack. I often use leftover rice or lentils and roll and steam the leaves for a tasty picnic lunch. You can also stuff the leaves with grilled vegetables or quinoa for the perfect finger food. Grape leaves act as a protector of the fruit; when their job is done they die, but this recipe brings them new life and is a lovely way to enjoy grape leaves outside of the summer season.

90 grape leaves

3 cups white wine vinegar

3 tablespoons kosher salt

Makes 3 pints

Assemble the canning stations as described on pages 5–7, steps 2–4. At the food preparation station, wash the grape leaves under cold running water and remove any leaves, or trim off pieces that are discolored. At the base of the leaf, clip the stems completely off with kitchen shears. Make an ice-water bath by placing cold water and 4 ice cubes into a medium bowl.

In a medium saucepan, bring 5 cups of water, vinegar, and salt to a boil over high heat. Once boiling, turn the heat to a low boil. In stacks of five, blanch the leaves in the vinegar-water for 30 seconds, flipping the stack after 15 seconds. Then remove the leaves with tongs as they turn olive in color and place them into the ice-water bath.

At the filling station, lay down 2 clean kitchen towels to absorb the liquid from the leaves. Remove the leaves one at a time and lay them on the towel. Stack one leaf on top of the other. Fold in half along the middle seam of the leaf. Roll the leaves into a cigar shape from top to stem. Remove the hot jars from the canning pot and stack rolled-up leaves into the jars by length, putting the top end of the roll into the bottom of the jar and leaving 1 inch of headspace. Depending on leaf size, pack between 11 and 15 bundles into each jar.

Using a heat-resistant pitcher, pour brine over the leaves, leaving ¼ inch of headspace, and press the leaves into the brine with a spoon. Remove air pockets, add brine if necessary, wipe the rim, and secure the lid. Place jars in the water bath, covered by 1 inch of water. Once the water is boiling, process for 10 minutes (pages 11–14, steps 7–12).

TIPS

For this recipe it is easiest to use small-mouth pint jars; that way, the rolled-up leaves have enough space to stand on end.

You can use these grape leaves in place of the beet leaves for the Beet Leaf Dolmas with Seeded Rice recipe (page 123).

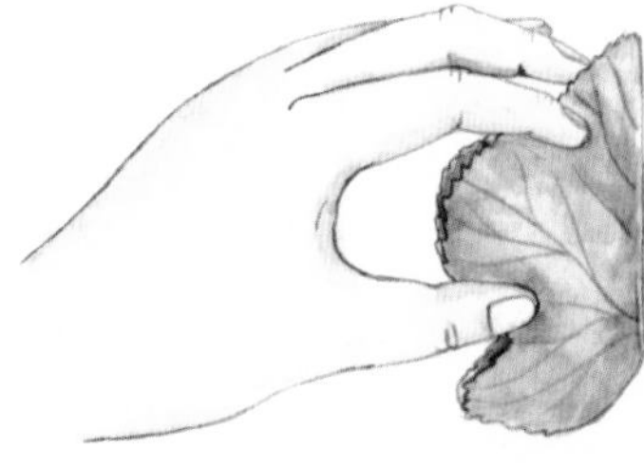

Stack one leaf on top of the other.
Fold in half along the middle seam.
Roll the leaves into a cigar shape from top to stem.

Recipe

BLUE CHEESE AND GRAPE BRIOCHE FLATBREAD

I don't usually bake, but I am inspired by Kristen Murray, the chef and owner of Måurice, a sweet little luncheonette in downtown Portland. Kristen can often be seen standing behind the counter making this brioche with love and care. She puts her heart into every plate and bite that comes out of her kitchen, which I also strive to do when I entertain guests at home. Brioche can sometimes be a little tricky to tackle, but nothing shows your love like this special treat. I start this bread the day before I need it, as it has an 18-hour rise time.

2 cups (4 sticks) unsalted butter, room temperature

3 cups (500 grams) all-purpose flour

⅓ cup (75 grams) granulated sugar

1 teaspoon (10 grams) sea salt

6 medium eggs, room temperature, divided

3 tablespoons (20 grams) fresh yeast

Olive oil, for rubbing down bowl

1 jar Tarragon Pickled Muscat Grapes (page 36)

¼ pound blue cheese

1 tablespoon fresh tarragon

Before starting, take out the butter from the refrigerator and cut it into ½-inch cubes. Let it sit out until it comes to room temperature, about 45 minutes.

In the metal bowl of a stand mixer, stir together the flour, sugar, and salt. Fit the mixer with a dough hook and lock both the bowl and the stand in place. Add the first egg and mix on low for 5 minutes, adding one egg at a time, but reserving one egg for later. Once each egg is incorporated into the dough, add another.

Place the yeast in a small glass bowl and add 1 teaspoon hot water. Mix with your fingers to form a paste. Add the paste to the mixing bowl and mix on low for 2 minutes.

Add butter gradually, a few cubes at a time, and wait until it's incorporated before adding additional butter. Stop the mixer and scrape down the bowl in between adding the cubes of butter. Once all the butter is in the bowl, mix on low for 35 minutes. The dough will be sticky and soft.

Rub a large mixing bowl with olive oil. Scrape the dough into the oiled bowl and cover with a kitchen towel. Allow the dough to double in size, rising at room temperature, for at least 12 hours.

Line a baking sheet with parchment paper. After the dough has risen, punch it down and put it onto the sheet. Form the dough into an 8 x 11 rectangle. Refrigerate for at least 6 hours.

Preheat the oven to 350°F.

Make an egg wash by whisking the remaining egg with a fork. Remove the dough from the refrigerator. It will be solid to the touch. Using a pastry brush, spread the egg wash evenly over the top of the brioche.

Drain the grapes and gently pat dry. Randomly arrange the grapes on top of the dough. Bake for 40 minutes, or until lightly golden. Remove and sprinkle with the blue cheese. Return to the oven for another 5 minutes, or until the cheese is melted.

Let the bread cool on a wire cooling rack. Garnish with fresh tarragon and cut into rectangles. Serve slightly warm.

TIPS

Baking measurements are included by weight in this recipe to ensure an accurate rise.

Fresh yeast can be purchased at specialty stores in the refrigerated section, or online (see Stocking Your Pantry on page 212).

Green Tomatoes

Green tomatoes are something every Portland gardener is familiar with. My family calls them "opportunities on the vine." We love green tomatoes and we have great ideas for using the surplus we are left with in September. Green tomatoes are full of vitamin C, and although often fried, there are many healthier and arguably tastier alternatives: pickles, sauces, and ketchup are some of my favorites. Some people with sensitivity to nightshades might want to avoid green tomatoes. Unlike their flavorful ripe red siblings, green tomatoes have little flavor and work best in highly spiced and seasoned recipes. Even though most people think of both green and red tomatoes as vegetables, they are indeed fruits.

TIP
You can use this Green Enchilada Sauce (page 47) in both the Smoked Chicken Enchiladas (page 48) and the Red Pork Posole with Beer (page 176).

Canned

GREEN TOMATO BLOODY MARY MIX

Our canning club sets up a yearly bloody Mary bar to celebrate our anniversary, and it's one of my favorite days of the year! Club members bring jars of pickled goods to add to the bar and build their own drinks. We set out long skewers and each guest can pack them full. Slightly spicy, flavorful, and fun, this recipe uses an abundance of green tomatoes and makes a great holiday gift. Simply mix one part vodka with three parts bloody Mary mix for the perfect green bloody Mary. Green tomatoes have a lower acidity than red, hence the addition of citric acid.

5 pounds green tomatoes (about 12 large tomatoes)

4 serrano peppers

1 head garlic

1 tablespoon extra virgin olive oil, for drizzling

2 tablespoons kosher salt

2 tablespoons wasabi powder

1½ tablespoons finely ground black pepper

1 tablespoon mustard powder

1 tablespoon celery seeds

1 teaspoon citric acid

½ teaspoon caraway seeds

½ teaspoon dried tarragon

½ teaspoon cayenne pepper

4 tablespoons Cucumber Mustard Hot Sauce (page 142)

4 tablespoons brine from Tiny Dill Zucchini Pickles (page 197)

½ cup fresh lime juice (from about 4 large limes)

Makes 6 pints

Preheat the oven to 350°F.

Assemble the canning stations as described on pages 5–7, steps 2–4. Wash the green tomatoes and slice into quarters. Wash the serrano peppers and pop off the stems.

Cut the top off the head of garlic and place it on a square of aluminum foil, drizzle with olive oil, and close up the foil. Place it on a baking sheet. Put the sheet in the center rack of the oven and roast for 60 minutes. Let the garlic cool and pop out the garlic cloves from the skin (put the skins into a freezer bag and use later for making the Liquid Gold Vegetable Stock on page 52).

Working in 2 batches, place half the tomatoes, all the garlic, and all the spices, seeds, and citric acid in a blender. Add ½ cup of water and blend on low until the tomatoes are smooth. Then turn to high and blend until no seeds are visible, about 3 minutes. For the second batch, blend the remaining tomatoes, hot sauce, pickle brine, and ½ cup of water.

In a large saucepan, add the blended mixtures. Heat on medium-high until bubbling. Reduce the heat to medium and let simmer, uncovered, for 5 minutes. Add the lime juice to the pot, stir, and turn the heat to the lowest setting.

At the filling station, keep the jars and mixture hot while filling each jar. Ladle the mix into a heat-resistant pitcher and use a funnel to fill each jar, leaving ¼ inch of headspace. Remove the air pockets, wipe the rim, and secure the lid. Place the jars in the water bath, covered by 1 inch of water. Once the water is boiling, process for 20 minutes (pages 11–14, steps 7–12).

TIPS

If you did not make the Cucumber Mustard Hot Sauce, use your favorite vinegar-based green hot sauce.

If you did not make the Tiny Dill Zucchini Pickles, use pickle brine from the fridge.

You can purchase citric acid from organic herb and spice retailers (see Stocking Your Pantry on page 212).

Canned

GREEN ENCHILADA SAUCE

Portland has a history of temperamental summers, which can lead to gardens full of unripe green tomatoes. Oregon gardeners watch and wait every year, hoping for just a few more sunny days. Sometimes we get them; most years we don't. As the rain starts to fall, we are all left with pounds and pounds of green tomatoes. If you don't struggle with the same drizzly Pacific Northwest weather that we do and find that all of your tomatoes ripen to a luscious bright red, count yourself lucky and substitute tomatillos for the green tomatoes. This sauce is tangy and slightly spicy, making it perfect for all palates. (See photo on page 43.)

4 pounds green tomatoes

12 jalapeño peppers

6 Anaheim peppers

2 medium onions

10 garlic cloves

½ cup fresh lime juice (from about 4 large limes)

2 tablespoons plus 2½ cups distilled vinegar, divided

1 tablespoon Mexican oregano

2 teaspoons kosher salt, divided

½ teaspoon ground cumin

Makes 8 pints

Assemble the canning stations as described on pages 5–7, steps 2–4. At the food preparation station, wash the green tomatoes, jalapeños, and Anaheim peppers. Core the tomatoes, removing any brown spots, and cut them into wedges. Remove the tops and seeds from the peppers and slice into large chunks. Peel and roughly slice the onions and garlic. Juice the limes (saving the peels in freezer bags for stuffing inside a roasting chicken).

At the stove station, heat 2 tablespoons vinegar in a large, nonreactive, heavy-bottom stockpot over medium-high heat. Add the onion and garlic. Stir occasionally for 5 minutes to avoid sticking and add ½ cup vinegar. Cook for 5 minutes, stirring occasionally. Add the peppers, 1 cup vinegar, Mexican oregano, 1 teaspoon salt, and cumin. Cook for 5 minutes, stirring continuously. Add the tomatoes, the remaining 1 teaspoon salt, and the remaining 1 cup vinegar. Cover with a lid and simmer for 12 minutes over low heat. Add the lime juice and blend the sauce with an immersion blender until smooth. Return to low heat.

At the filling station, keep the jars and sauce hot while filling each jar. Use a funnel and a heat-resistant pitcher to fill the jars, leaving ½ inch of headspace. Remove the air pockets, wipe the rim, and secure the lid. Place the jars in the water bath, covered by 1 inch of water. Once the water is boiling, process for 10 minutes (pages 11–14, steps 7–12).

TIP

Mexican oregano can be found in the Latin food aisle at most grocery stores. It has earthy flavors similar to Mediterranean oregano, with the addition of citrus and floral elements. If you can't find it, substitute with Greek oregano.

Preserved

BASIL AND TOMATO LEAF ICE CREAM

When I was growing up, summertime meant that my parents would break out their ice cream maker, one of those gadgets from the '70s with the crank handle. Inspired by David Lebovitz (author of *My Paris Kitchen*), these instructions are specific to a no-gadget ice cream making process but are adaptable, so whether you have a hand-crank machine or a super-fancy ice cream maker, you can make this recipe happen. Tomato leaves and fresh basil give this ice cream the essence of a summer garden, paired with just the icy-cool blast you need to beat the summer heat. Use this technique with any of your favorite herbs and edible flowers for a taste of summer year-round.

½ cup fresh basil leaves, loosely packed

1 cup tomato leaves, loosely packed

3 cups heavy whipping cream

⅔ cup granulated sugar

¼ teaspoon kosher salt

5 egg yolks

Makes 1 quart

At the food preparation station, wash the basil and tomato leaves. Keeping the basil and tomato leaves separate, chiffonade them into ribbons.

In a medium saucepan, simmer the cream, sugar, salt, and tomato leaves over low heat, stirring occasionally, for 10 minutes.

(CONTINUED)

(CONTINUED)

Remove the pot from the heat and let the contents infuse and cool for 10 minutes.

In a medium bowl, whisk together the egg yolks until creamy. Continue whisking and slowly add the cream mixture from the pot. Once combined, put the contents back into the pot, cook on medium-low heat, whisking occasionally for 20 minutes, until the mixture thickens enough to coat a wooden spoon.

Prepare an ice-water bath by placing a medium bowl into another large bowl filled halfway with ice and water.

Pour the mixture through a fine-mesh strainer into the top bowl and stir until cool, about 10 minutes. Stir in the basil leaves. Pour into a 2-quart glass baking dish. Freeze for 30 minutes, then stir with a spatula and scrape the sides, giving it a good mix. Place the dish back in the freezer for 30 minutes, scrape the sides, and stir together; place the dish back into the freezer for another 30 minutes. Repeat this process for 2 to 3 hours, until the desired consistency is achieved. Store in the freezer, covered with plastic wrap against the ice cream, for up to 6 months.

TIPS

Use farm-fresh eggs and full-fat cream to achieve maximum flavor.

Garnish with fresh strawberries for a full summer blast.

NOTE

Despite what you may have heard, tomato leaves are not actually poisonous; you'd have to consume at least a pound and a half to experience a negative side effect. Still, consuming tomato leaves is not for everyone, so if you'd like, feel free to replace with a summer herb of your choice.

Recipe

SMOKED CHICKEN ENCHILADAS

Smoked chicken enchiladas are my go-to dish for potlucks. These are gluten-free and can easily be made vegetarian by substituting smoked tofu for the chicken. We live next to a Russian meat market and they smoke chickens daily. When I walk by the market to take my daughter to the park, and catch the delicious wafting smells escaping from the smoker, I know instantly that we are making these smoked chicken enchiladas for dinner. I like using a stacking method (as opposed to rolling the enchiladas) when making mine, because it is quick and easy.

4 smoked chicken thighs

2 cups mozzarella cheese

1 cup cotija cheese

1 pint Green Enchilada Sauce (page 47), divided

2 cups Mexican crema

15 corn tortillas

½ teaspoon Mexican oregano

2 tablespoons fresh cilantro, chopped

Preheat the oven to 375°F.

At the preparation station, peel off the skin from the chicken and remove the meat from the bones. Cut the chicken into ½-inch pieces. Shred the mozzarella cheese and cotija with a box grater. Mix ½ cup of the Green Enchilada Sauce with Mexican crema.

Spread ½ cup of the crema mixture over the bottom of a 4-quart glass baking pan. Arrange five tortillas over the sauce, completely covering the bottom of the pan. Tear the tortillas if necessary to completely cover the bottom of the pan. Spoon more crema mixture over the tortillas and sprinkle with half the chicken pieces. Cover with half of a mixture of both cheeses. Cover with five tortillas, creating an even surface. Spread the remaining crema mixture and sprinkle with the remaining chicken. Cover with the remaining five tortillas and add the remaining enchilada sauce and cheese. Sprinkle the top with Mexican oregano.

Bake the enchiladas uncovered for 40 minutes, or until the cheese is melted and bubbling on the sides. Let the pan sit for 10 minutes to set. Sprinkle with chopped cilantro and serve.

TIPS

You can save the bones and skins for making a smoked chicken stock; store them in a bag in the freezer until you are ready to make the stock.

If you did not make the Green Enchilada Sauce, substitute with your favorite enchilada sauce.

You can substitute smoked chicken breasts for the thighs if you prefer white meat.

Mexican crema can be found in the dairy section of specialty grocery stores. It is also known as Mexican sour cream. If you can't find it, substitute with regular sour cream.

Kumquats

These charming little fruits have become part of our holiday tradition—we find them Christmas morning packed into our stockings with tangerines and whole walnuts. Although not typically an Oregon fruit, we can easily source kumquats from our neighboring states. Pacific Northwest indoor gardeners also have luck growing kumquats. The tiny, oval fruits are eaten whole (which create zero food waste!) and leave a surprising zing in your mouth. The outer peel is sour and full of essential oils, while the inside is sweet.

Canned

SAVORY KUMQUAT MARMALADE

This savory marmalade will become your kitchen condiment hero. I use it often and it adds a rich punch to any dish, from sweet to savory. I love stirring a spoonful into soups and stews and I especially love to use it in vinaigrettes for drizzling over fresh tomato salads. It has a nice Thai influence with the addition of the ginger, lemongrass, and chilies. The natural pectin in the kumquat rinds helps to thicken up this marmalade, but be careful not to let the heat get too high or the marmalade will caramelize.

¼ cup fresh lime juice (from about 2 large limes)

2 pounds kumquats, sliced (about 4 cups)

2 medium shallots

2 large garlic cloves

2-inch piece of ginger, peeled, finely minced

¼ cup lemongrass (about 3 stalks)

2 Thai chilies

2 cups granulated sugar

2 tablespoons kosher salt

2 tablespoons white wine vinegar

Makes 5 half-pints

Assemble the canning stations as described on pages 5–7, steps 2–4. Juice the limes and compost the skins (or save them in freezer bags). Wash the kumquats and slice into ¼-inch slices from stem to end and remove the seeds with the tip of a knife. Peel the shallots and garlic, and mince them.

Cut off the ends of the lemongrass and remove the 2 outer layers; set aside all lemongrass scraps for the Liquid Gold Vegetable Stock recipe on page 52. Slice the inner lemongrass stalk into thin slices. Wash and slice the Thai chilies into thin slices.

In a large, heavy-bottom skillet, place the kumquats, sugar, salt and 4 cups of water. Bring to a boil over high heat. Once boiling, reduce the heat to a medium simmer over low heat, let the fruit bubble, stirring occasionally to keep it from caramelizing, about 30 minutes.

Meanwhile, heat the vinegar, lemongrass, shallots, ginger, and garlic in a medium skillet over medium-high heat, stirring occasionally for 6 minutes, or until soft. Stir in the Thai chilies and lime juice. Add the contents of the skillet to the marmalade pot after it has cooked for 30 minutes. Stir to combine and simmer on low for 5 to 15 minutes, stirring occasionally. The marmalade is done when it coats the back of a spoon.

At the filling station, keep the jars and marmalade hot while filling each jar. Use a funnel and a large spoon to fill each jar, leaving ¼ inch of headspace. Remove the air pockets, wipe the rim, and secure the lid. Place the jars in the water bath, covered by 1 inch of water. Once the water is boiling, process for 10 minutes (pages 11–14, steps 7–12).

TIP

If you have a kumquat tree, you can dry the leaves and use them for tea.

Canned

PICKLED KUMQUATS AND PISTACHIOS

While working at a night market one evening, I glanced over and saw my friend Camille snacking on tiny oranges. I exclaimed, "Are you eating whole oranges?" She gave me one and told me to eat the whole thing very quickly, so I popped it in my mouth and bit down. All at once I felt orange oil explode inside my mouth and I began chewing until the sting of the tart oil was eased by the sweet inside. I have been chomping on these beauties ever since. Camille has a honey business called Old Blue Raw Honey, and I created this recipe using her coriander varietal honey, which is my favorite.

2 pounds kumquats

4 cups apple cider vinegar

3 tablespoons Orange Peel Pickling Spice (page 75)

1 tablespoon kosher salt

¾ cup unsalted shelled pistachios

1 tablespoon local honey

Makes 6 half-pints

Assemble the canning stations as described on pages 5–7, steps 2–4. At the food preparation station, wash the kumquats under cold running water, pull off any stems, and compost or eat any kumquats that are soft. Slice the kumquats in half lengthwise and remove any seeds with the tip of a knife.

In a medium, stainless steel saucepan, heat the vinegar, 1 cup of water, Orange Peel Pickling Spice,

(CONTINUED)

(CONTINUED)

and salt over high heat, until boiling. Turn down heat to a low simmer, add the pistachios and honey, and infuse for 5 minutes.

At the filling station, keep the jars and brine hot while filling each jar. Cold-pack the fruit into each jar, leaving 1 inch of headspace. Pour the brine into each jar, ensuring that both pistachios and spices go into each one and leaving ½ inch of headspace. Remove the air pockets, add brine if necessary, wipe the rim, and secure the lid. Place the jars in the water bath, covered by 1 inch of water. Once the water is boiling, process for 10 minutes (pages 11–14, steps 7–12).

TIP

The brine on this is a bit cloudy, which is a result of the nut proteins releasing into the liquid. Be sure to drain the brine before serving, saving it to use in the Kumquat Pistachio Chicken with Coconut Black Sesame Rice recipe (page 54).

Preserved

LIQUID GOLD VEGETABLE STOCK

I use vegetable scraps for my stock; as I cook in the kitchen, I put leftover scraps like lemon rinds, garlic skins, and turmeric peels in freezer bags, and when it seems like I have enough, I boil them all together. This is less of a recipe and more of a suggestion to do the same. You can also make it with fresh vegetables. Since this recipe isn't canned, you can throw in whatever you have. The addition of the turmeric peels makes this stock a glowing orange—like liquid gold.

1½ pounds yellow onions

1 pound celery

½ pound carrots

1 cup turmeric peels (reserved from Turmeric Mustard, page 188)

1 cup lemongrass stalks and ends (reserved from Savory Kumquat Marmalade, page 51)

6 garlic cloves

2 tablespoons kosher salt

1 tablespoon dried thyme

1 tablespoon dried oregano

Makes 4 quarts

In a large, stainless steel stockpot fitted with a lid, place 20 cups of water and all the ingredients. Bring to a boil over high heat. Once boiling, lower the heat to medium and cover; simmer for 2 hours, turning the heat down as needed.

Strain the stock through a fine-mesh strainer into a large, heat-resistant pitcher.

Fill quart jars, leaving 2 inches of headspace and freeze or store in the refrigerator for up to 5 days.

TIP

You can use this stock in the recipes for Dan Dan Noodles (page 146), Tomato Bisque with Crab (page 104), Oven-Roasted Chicken Thighs with Pickled Tomatoes (page 107), and Habañero Meatballs with Cauliflower Rice (page 83).

Kumquat Pistachio Chicken with Coconut Black Sesame Rice, page 54.

Recipe

KUMQUAT PISTACHIO CHICKEN WITH COCONUT BLACK SESAME RICE

Kumquats are a small citrus fruit with a very short season. Canning becomes imperative to prolong a brief moment in time and enjoy the fruit later in the year. This dish then becomes really special, because you have preserved such a rare ingredient. The browning process when cooking the chicken achieves a depth of flavor that is highlighted by the brightness and acidity of the kumquats. (See photo on page 53.)

1 cup white rice

1 cup coconut milk

1 tablespoon black sesame seeds

1 tablespoon kosher salt

2 teaspoons sesame oil, divided

¼ cup fresh lime juice (from 2 large limes)

1 stalk lemongrass

1 tablespoon granulated sugar

2 medium shallots

2 garlic cloves

1 red Fresno chili pepper

4 chicken breasts, boneless and skinless

1 tablespoon Lemon Peel Spice Rub (page 61)

1 half-pint jar Pickled Kumquats and Pistachios (page 51), divided

2 tablespoons coconut oil

2 tablespoons cilantro, chopped

Makes 4 servings

In a medium saucepan with a fitted lid, toast the rice over medium-high heat, shaking the pan back and forth every 30 seconds for 4 minutes, until fragrant. Add 1 cup of water (it may splatter a bit). Add the coconut milk, sesame seeds, and salt. Bring to a boil over high heat. Once boiling, stir in 1 teaspoon of sesame oil. Reduce the heat to a low simmer and cover. Cook for 20 minutes.

At the food preparation station, juice the limes. Prepare the lemongrass by trimming off the ends, peeling off the outer three layers, and chopping into ⅛-inch-thick slices. In a small bowl, stir the lemongrass, lime juice, and sugar; set aside. Peel and mince the shallots and garlic. Slice the chili into ¼-inch rings. Cut the chicken into 1-inch cubes. Sprinkle the chicken with the Lemon Peel Spice Rub. Drain the Pickled Kumquats and Pistachios pickling brine through a fine-mesh strainer; set aside. Brush off whole spices from the kumquats and pistachios.

Heat the coconut oil in a medium skillet over medium-high heat. Once the oil is hot and fluid, place the chicken pieces evenly in the pan. Let them sit untouched for 6 minutes to brown. Check one piece; if it's brown, flip the chicken cubes. Let them sit untouched for another 6 minutes to brown.

Add the shallots and garlic, and stir until soft. Add in the lemongrass mixture, 2 tablespoons pickling brine (from the Pickled Kumquats and Pistachios), pistachios, and kumquats. Heat until bubbly, about 2 minutes.

Turn heat off and add chili peppers. Fluff the rice with a fork and drizzle in the remaining 1 teaspoon sesame oil. Serve chicken and sauce over rice. Garnish with cilantro.

TIPS

If you did not make the Lemon Peel Spice Rub, replace it with your favorite chicken rub.

If you did not make the Pickled Kumquats and Pistachios, use fresh quantities of both, and add 5 minutes' sautéing time.

Lemons

It is possible to grow lemons and other citrus in Oregon, although it takes a bit of planning and moving trees indoors and out. There are a few farms that follow this painstaking process for us, resulting in local organic citrus. In my sauce kitchen, I often use lemon and lime juice in our canning process to help create an acidic environment and it gives my recipes a nice brightness. When cooking in my home kitchen, I use citrus to keep fruits and vegetables from browning—a true necessity. Canned lemons are often preserved with lots of sugar, but in the following recipes I have chosen to safely decrease the sugar and let the tart lemon shine without suffocating its natural bite. Lemon peels are packed with fiber and restore pH balance naturally to the body. This chapter incorporates the peels into a spice rub that can be easily added to meals, saving wasted food and nourishing your body all at once.

Canned

LEMON PICKLED MUSTARD SEEDS

I like to think of this recipe as vegan white caviar, not to be confused with Britain's white caviar, which is composed of snail eggs. These pickled seeds bring a wonderful pop to sandwiches and salads, and you can use them in place of roe or caviar in recipes. The coriander adds a lovely floral perfume that interacts nicely with the bite of the mustard seeds. If you are not a fan of coriander, you can leave it out and replace it with brown mustard seeds.

½ cup yellow mustard seeds

4 tablespoons coriander seeds

¼ cup fresh lemon juice, plus the rind (from about 1 large lemon)

½ cup champagne vinegar

1 tablespoon local honey

1 teaspoon kosher salt

Makes 4 quarter-pints

Assemble the canning stations as described on pages 5–7, steps 2–4. At the food preparation station, soak the mustard seeds and coriander seeds in cold running water for 10 minutes; drain through a fine-mesh strainer or cheesecloth. Wash the lemon and remove the peel without the pith. Slice the peel into ribbons. Cut the lemon in half and juice.

In a medium saucepan, add the champagne vinegar, ¼ cup of water, lemon juice, honey, and salt. Infuse over low heat for 8 minutes, until hot and bubbly. Add the seeds to the brine and heat over medium-high for 5 minutes.

At the filling station, keep the jars and contents hot while filling each jar. Pour the mixture through a fine-mesh strainer over a heat-resistant pitcher to catch the brine. Spoon the seeds into the jars and place the lemon rind along the inside edge, so that it's visible from the outside. Fill, leaving 1½ inch of headspace. Then top with the brine to ½ inch of headspace. Push the lemon rind down with a chopstick. Remove the air pockets, add brine to cover, wipe the rim, and secure the lid. Place the jars in the water bath, covered by 1 inch of water. Once the water is boiling, process for 10 minutes (pages 11–14, steps 7–12).

TIPS

Make sure to follow the headspace directions, as the seeds will expand a bit during the canning process

Use this recipe to make the Ahi Tuna Canapé (page 61).

Canned

VANILLA BEAN LEMONADE

We do not see citrus at the Portland Farmers Market, but it is pretty easy to source from our California neighbors. I love to hear our friends' stories of visiting their relatives with citrus trees in their gardens, and bringing an extra bag with them when they travel south to fill with fruit to bring back to Portland. This recipe is slightly sweet, very tart, and has the fragrant aroma of vanilla. After the lemonade is processed, mix it on a 1:1 ratio with water, sparkling water, or sparkling wine.

7 cups fresh lemon juice (from about 35 medium lemons)

1 vanilla bean

1½ cups granulated sugar

Makes 6 pints

Assemble the canning stations as described on pages 5–7, steps 2–4. At the food preparation station, wash the lemons under cold running water. Roll the lemons on the counter, back and forth, pressing slightly. Peel off the rinds with a sharp knife and save them for the Lemon Peel Spice Rub recipe on page 61. Cut the lemons in half and juice with a citrus juicer. Cut the vanilla bean in half from top to bottom. Scrape the inside of the pod with a sharp knife, saving the seeds.

In a large, stainless steel pot, place the lemon juice, 3 cups of water, sugar, vanilla bean pod, and seeds. Cook over medium heat until the sugar is dissolved,

(CONTINUED)

(CONTINUED)

stirring occasionally, about 5 minutes. Pour the liquid through a fine-mesh strainer into a heat-resistant pitcher.

At the filling station, keeping the jars and lemonade hot, fill the jars using a funnel, leaving ¼ inch of headspace. Wipe each rim and secure the lids. Place the jars in the water bath, covered by 1 inch of water. Once the water is boiling, process for 10 minutes (pages 11–14, steps 7–12).

TIPS

Using room-temperature lemons and rolling them on the counter before juicing helps to extract more juice from the citrus.

If you don't have a vanilla bean, substitute with 2 teaspoons vanilla extract.

Save what is left of the lemons and store in the freezer to stuff inside a chicken to roast.

You can use this lemonade to make the Sparkling Wine Poached Pears (page 86) and the Party Punch (page 208).

Preserved

ORANGE BLOSSOM LEMON CURD

My mom is a huge fan of lemon curd, and this recipe is one of her favorites. I make it for Mother's Day and her birthday. It is perfect spooned over olive oil pound cake or simply spread onto toast. This complex creation contains aromatics from an orange blossom and tartness from a citrus, all mixed together in a decadent, creamy curd. Making curd can be a fragile practice, the biggest concern being accidentally turning the mixture into cooked eggs. Watch the heat and stir constantly to achieve desired results. This recipe requires a lot of stirring, so get those arms ready to work!

¼ cup fresh lemon juice (from 2 large lemons), plus zest

¼ cup fresh lime juice (from 3 large limes), plus zest

12 egg yolks, room temperature

1 tablespoon orange blossom water

½ cup (1 stick) unsalted butter, room temperature

¼ cup extra virgin coconut oil

½ cup local honey

Makes 1 pint

Assemble the canning stations as described on pages 5–7, steps 2–4. At the food preparation station, wash the lemons and limes under cold running water. With a zester, zest the lemons and limes, avoiding the white pith. Cut the citrus in half and extract the juice with a citrus juicer.

Prepare a double boiler: Stack a medium, heat-resistant, glass bowl on top of a medium saucepan (filled with 3 cups of water). Make sure the base of the bowl fits snuggly, while the sides of the bowl hang over the pot.

Separate the egg yolks and whites and remove any fibrous pieces from the yolk (you can save the whites for vegetable omelets). In a glass bowl, whisk together the lemon juice, lime juice, egg yolks, zest, and orange blossom water until thoroughly mixed.

Bring the water to a boil over high heat. Turn the heat to a low simmer. Place the bowl of whisked eggs on top of the pot, stirring constantly with a spatula for 5 minutes. Add the butter and stir for another 5 minutes. Add the coconut oil and stir for 5 minutes. Slowly drizzle in the honey and begin whisking for 5 to 10 minutes, until thick. Remove from the heat and run through a fine-mesh strainer to remove any zest or curdled egg.

At the filling station, use a funnel and a ladle to fill each jar with curd, leaving ¼ inch of headspace. Remove the air pockets by tapping the jar gently, wipe the rim, and secure the lid. Store the curd in the refrigerator for up to 1 week, or in the freezer for up to a year.

TIP

Orange blossom water can be found at specialty grocery stores and is made from fresh blossoms from a bitter orange (see Stocking Your Pantry on page 212).

TIP
These Ahi Tuna Canapes are best served right away.

Preserved

LEMON PEEL SPICE RUB

My father-in-law makes perfect roast chicken on the barbecue. It took a few nudges for him to tell me his secret, but he eventually revealed that he used a store-bought spice blend, which is full of preservatives. Right away, I went to work developing a spice rub using only natural ingredients that would taste better. We taste-tested them side by side and I'm happy to say that this blend is officially Dad-approved. As a bonus, it is also a great way to use up any leftover lemon peels after making the Vanilla Bean Lemonade (page 56).

Zest from 3 lemons (or zest reserved from the Turmeric Ginger Juice Shots recipe, page 189)

1 tablespoon granulated sugar

2 tablespoons kosher salt

1 tablespoon paprika

1 teaspoon celery seeds

½ teaspoon granulated onion powder

½ teaspoon granulated garlic powder

¼ teaspoon turmeric powder

¼ teaspoon cayenne pepper

Makes 4 tablespoons

Preheat the oven to 200°F.

Line a baking sheet with parchment paper. Zest the lemons with a box grater. Sprinkle the lemon zest evenly across the paper. Place into the center of the oven for 8 minutes. After 8 minutes, crush the zest between your fingers and sprinkle across the paper. Return to the oven for 10 minutes. Crush again, and return for 10 minutes. The lemon zest is done when it is dry and still yellow in color. Remove from the oven and let it cool.

Grind the sugar and all the spices, together with the lemon zest, in a mortar and pestle or a spice grinder until fine. Store in a glass vessel and keep in a cool dry place for up to 6 months.

TIPS

Watch the lemon peels closely as they bake. They brown quickly and, if overcooked, they will be bitter.

Use this spice rub to make the Kumquat Pistachio Chicken with Coconut Black Sesame Rice (page 54) and the Oven-Roasted Chicken Thighs with Pickled Tomatoes (page 107).

Recipe

AHI TUNA CANAPÉ

A canapé is a party snack that is easy to eat in one bite. These appetizers are best when they are simple, beautiful, and fresh. This perfect combination is a fun way to make an impressive start for your next gathering. Be sure to buy the best quality Ahi from your local fishmonger. The pickled mustard seeds add a bright lemony pop and textural complexity to the fresh, delicate tuna. As an added bonus, the prep time for this is short, so you can spend extra time chatting with your friends.

1 medium cucumber

½ pound Ahi tuna steak

1 tablespoon soy sauce

1 tablespoon sesame oil

½-inch piece ginger, peeled and grated

¼ teaspoon crushed red pepper flakes

1 teaspoon fresh chives

1 jar Lemon Pickled Mustard Seeds (page 56)

Makes 14 canapés

TIP

If you did not make the Lemon Pickled Mustard Seeds, replace with caviar.

Wash the cucumber and slice into ¼-inch-thick whole rounds. Using a sharp knife, cut the tuna into ½-inch cubes. In a medium bowl, whisk the soy sauce, sesame oil, ginger, and crushed red pepper flakes. Add the tuna and gently coat with the sauce.

Top each slice of cucumber with a heaping amount of dressed tuna. Garnish with chives and Lemon Pickled Mustard Seeds.

Mangoes

Mangoes are one of the tropical fruits that just can't grow in Oregon. However, it is quite easy to get them from organic markets, mostly sourced from the Caribbean. I love the velvety texture ripe mangoes add to sauces and jams; they elevate canning products with their elegant status. This chapter highlights mangoes in both their ripe and unripe states—both equally decadent and packed with vitamin C. Mango peels and seeds are often ground into amchoor powder and incorporated into dishes to promote healthy digestion. Mango consumers often discard the peels, leaving behind nutrients that come carb-free, unlike the flesh of the fruit—so save those precious peels.

Mango, Rose Petal, and Saffron Jam, page 64.

Canned

MANGO, ROSE PETAL, AND SAFFRON JAM

I love making this luxurious jam for baby showers. It is beautiful and lovely, and every part of the process makes me feel excited about the person I am gifting it to. Mangoes feel extravagant, and the rose petals and saffron make them over-the-top elegant. Gathering the ingredients, prepping, cooking, and canning this jam makes me feel as though I am creating a perfume fit for a queen. Saffron threads come from the stamens of a flower that blooms one week a year. They enhance the golden color of the mango and bring another floral element to the rose water. (See photo on page 63.)

7 ripe champagne mangoes (about 2 pounds once cut)

½ cup fresh lemon juice (from about 3 lemons)

¼ teaspoon saffron threads

3 cups granulated sugar

2 teaspoons pink rose petals

2 teaspoons rose water

Makes 6 half-pints

Assemble the canning stations as described on pages 5–7, steps 2–4. At the food preparation station, wash the mangoes under cold running water to remove any sticky residue. Using a sharp paring knife, remove the fruit from the skins and the seeds, and set the skins aside for the Pickled Mango Peel recipe on page 67.

In a large, shallow, heavy-bottom skillet, combine the mango flesh, the mango seeds, lemon juice, and saffron. Cook over medium heat, stirring occasionally to avoid sticking, until soft; the pieces of mango should gently mash apart with a wooden spoon after about 8 minutes. Remove the seeds with tongs and compost. Add the sugar and stir to combine. Cook for 10 minutes, stirring regularly to avoid burning. Turn down the heat if the mixture begins to bubble rapidly; avoid overheating or the jam will become dark and caramelized. Turn off the heat, sprinkle in the rose petals and rose water, and gently fold into the jam.

At the filling station, keep the jars and the jam hot. Use a funnel and a ladle to fill each jar with jam, leaving ¼ inch of headspace. Remove the air pockets, wipe the rims, and secure the lids. Place the jars in the water bath, covered by 1 inch of water. Once the water is boiling, process for 10 minutes (pages 11–14, steps 7–12).

TIPS

If the mangoes are not ripe, they will not break down into the jam. If this is the case, dice the mango flesh into ¼-inch pieces once it is separated from the seed. The result will be a chunkier marmalade style jam.

Use this recipe to make the Mango Masa Tart (page 68).

Canned

MANGO BARBECUE SAUCE

My daughter loves to dip everything she eats into sauces. In fact, two of her first five words were chip and dip. This mildly spiced sauce is a particular favorite of my little sauce connoisseur. In contrast to commercially produced sauces—which often contain corn syrup and other preservatives—I use organic produce and ingredients instead. That means my daughter can lick the plate to her heart's content, and I can watch her worry-free. This recipe is also special because it doesn't use tomatoes, but the luscious texture may fool you into thinking it does.

1 pound yellow onions (about 2 cups)

4 garlic cloves

3 red bell peppers

2 pounds ripe mangoes (about 4 cups prepped)

3 cups distilled vinegar, divided

½-inch piece fresh ginger, peeled, finely minced

1 tablespoon kosher salt

1 teaspoon cayenne pepper

1 teaspoon sweet paprika

½ teaspoon ground cinnamon

½ teaspoon smoked paprika

⅓ cup molasses

⅔ cup light brown sugar, loosely packed

Makes 8 half-pints

Assemble the canning stations as described on pages 5–7, steps 2–4. At the food preparation station, peel and slice the onions and garlic. Wash the red bell peppers (compost the stem and seeds) and cut into large chunks. Peel the mangoes and remove the flesh from the seeds.

In a large saucepan over medium heat, place 1 cup distilled vinegar, onions, and garlic. Once the pan is hot, sauté for about 6 minutes, or until the onions begin to soften and the liquid has evaporated. Add 1 cup vinegar, ginger, red peppers, mangoes, salt, and spices. Simmer uncovered for 12 minutes, stirring occasionally, until the peppers are soft.

Working in 2 batches, pour ½ cup vinegar into a blender. Scrape half the contents of the pot into the blender. Blend on high until completely smooth. Pour the remaining ½ cup vinegar into the blender and the remaining contents of the pot, blending until completely smooth. Return to the pot and add the molasses and brown sugar. Over low heat, simmer and stir for 15 minutes; the sauce should be bubbling slightly.

At the filling station, keep the jars and sauce hot while filling each jar. Use a funnel and a heat-resistant pitcher to pour the sauce into the jar, leaving ½ inch of headspace. Remove the air pockets, wipe the rim, and secure the lid. Place the jars in the water bath, covered by 1 inch of water. Once the water is boiling, process for 10 minutes (pages 11–14, steps 7–12).

TIP
Using both sweet and smoked paprika in this recipe helps to achieve a balance of flavors.

TIP
Since you are eating the skins in this recipe, it is very important to purchase organic mangoes, or mangoes you are sure have not been sprayed with chemicals.

Preserved

PICKLED MANGO PEEL

I share a commercial kitchen with my friend Neha Petal. She is the owner of Masala Pop, an Indian-spiced popcorn company. We have become fast friends and supporters of each other's businesses. Every June, as the kids are wrapping up school, Neha's parents travel from the East Coast to spend time with the family, and with them they bring a suitcase full of homemade Indian spiced pickles. Eating her mom's beautiful pickles is my favorite start to every summer! Mango pickles are traditionally made with green, unripe mangoes. The peels are left on and soften in the process. I also add in any extra mango peels left over from making the other mango recipes.

1 whole green organic mango

1 cup organic mango peels (about 2 mangoes, reserved from Mango, Rose Petal, and Saffron Jam, page 64)

2 garlic cloves

¼ cup fresh lime juice (from about 2 limes)

1 tablespoon brown mustard seeds

¼ cup sunflower oil

1 teaspoon fenugreek (methi) seeds

½ teaspoon fennel seeds

1 teaspoon crushed red pepper flakes

1 teaspoon red pepper powder (kashmini)

1 teaspoon cayenne pepper

1 teaspoon citric acid

1½ teaspoons kosher salt, plus more to taste

¼ teaspoon asafoetida powder

¼ teaspoon turmeric powder

Makes 6 quarter-pints

At the preparation station, wash the mango under cold running water. Remove any black or discolored peel and compost it, leaving the rest of the green peel on. Peel and finely mince the garlic. Slice the limes in half and juice with a citrus juicer, placing the juice into a large bowl.

Toast the mustard seeds in a small dry skillet over medium heat, shaking the pan frequently, about 4 minutes, or until the seeds just start to pop. Pour the seeds into a small bowl and add the sunflower oil and garlic. Set the bowl aside to cool.

Slice each side off the mango and cut into ½-inch cubes, leaving the peel on. Cut off the remaining mango from the seed and cube the flesh. Place the mango cubes into the bowl of lime juice to keep them from browning. Cut the mango peels into ⅛-inch pieces. Toss the mangoes and peels in the lime juice until evenly coated.

Grind the fenugreek seeds, fennel seeds, and crushed red pepper flakes with a mortar and pestle or spice grinder. Add the ground mixture, red pepper powder, cayenne pepper, citric acid, salt, asafoetida, and turmeric powder to the bowl of mangoes. Mix well. Add in the oil mixture and mix until evenly coated. Cover closely with plastic wrap to minimize air contact and let sit in a warm spot in the kitchen for 24 hours. Stir and add salt to taste. Store in a clean glass jar and refrigerate for up to 2 weeks.

TIPS

The finer you dice the mango peels, the better the texture will be. If you want to make this recipe without using mango peels, substitute with one whole mango.

Asafoetida is a dried resin from the root of a tree. It is often found in recipes from south India and can be purchased in international grocery stores or online retailers (see Stocking Your Pantry on page 212).

Recipe

MANGO MASA TART

Masa harina, a corn flour made from lime-soaked corn kernels, is often used for making tortillas. The polenta and masa give this tart a nice crunch and texture, and it's a great recipe to make with any little people you know, because kids love to get in there and mix the batter with their hands. The steps are simple and easy enough for a fun and quick kitchen project, and the recipe is a great way to use up any jam you have in the pantry if you didn't make the Mango, Rose Petal, and Saffron Jam (page 64).

2 eggs, divided

½ cup all-purpose unbleached flour

½ cup masa harina

¼ cup polenta

¼ teaspoon kosher salt

½ cup (1 stick) salted butter, room temperature

⅓ cup granulated sugar

2 half-pints Mango, Rose Petal, and Saffron Jam (page 64)

½ teaspoon dried rose petals

Makes 1 tart

Separate one egg, saving the white to use later in the recipe. In a medium bowl, whisk the flour, masa harina, polenta, and salt, until evenly combined.

In a large bowl, cream together the butter and sugar until smooth. Add one whole egg and the egg yolk, whisking into the butter and the sugar. Add in the dry mix by hand one cup at a time, adding more as the dough comes together. Form the dough into a ball and refrigerate for 1 hour.

Preheat the oven to 350°F.

Grease the inside of a tart pan. Place the dough into the tart pan and press down to form an indent in the dough, which you will later fill with jam. Using a pastry brush, brush the dough with the leftover beaten egg white.

Place the tart pan on a baking sheet and bake in the center rack of the oven for 12 minutes. Pull out the tart and add the jam, spread evenly, and bake for another 5 minutes, until the jam bubbles and the crust is golden.

Let the jam set for 5 minutes. Top the tart with dried rose petals.

TIP

Use a small square tin to evenly indent the inside of the tart.

Oranges

In the winter you can find oranges at our natural food stores, and they are a lovely relief from the abundance of kale and root vegetables we pick up at the market. Both the flesh and the peels provide us with the vitamin C we need to fight off those nasty cold and flu symptoms. These beautiful citrus fruits brighten up our dreary winters right when we need it most. I love using oranges in sauces to add a nice body and also a bitter element from the pith. I encourage you to explore the many varieties of oranges. My favorites are blood oranges, cara cara, and satsumas. This chapter encourages you to eat and preserve the orange peel to both fight food waste and enjoy the vitamins within.

Orange Slices in Bergamot Syrup, page 72.

Canned

ORANGE SLICES IN BERGAMOT SYRUP

My mom used to drink orgeat (almond) lattes. Now, any time I smell delicate almond in the air I think of my mom, and that's probably why I put almond into so many of my recipes. The cara cara oranges called for in this recipe have beautiful red flesh and are low in acid, so make sure to add a touch of lemon. Bergamot tea is a black tea blend made from bergamot oranges, which are yellow in color and have a sour flavor. All the components come together here to make this wonderfully decadent delight. (See photo page 71.)

6 medium cara cara oranges, divided

2 bergamot tea bags

1½ cups cane sugar

1 teaspoon almond extract

1 tablespoon fresh lemon juice

Makes 6 half-pints

Assemble the canning stations as described on pages 5–7, steps 2–4. At the preparation station, wash the oranges under cold running water. Juice 2 oranges to extract ¾ cup of juice. Cut the remaining oranges in half from stem to end, set flat-side down, and slice into ⅛-inch half-moons.

In a medium saucepan, place 1 ½ cups of water, tea bags, cane sugar, almond extract, orange juice, and lemon juice. Bring to a simmer over medium heat, stirring to dissolve the sugar; simmer for 4 minutes, until golden in color. Once the sugar is dissolved, turn the heat to the lowest setting and remove the tea bags, squeezing out the liquid.

At the filling station, keep the jars and syrup hot while filling each jar. Pour the syrup into a heat-resistant pitcher. Filling one jar at a time, pour ¼ inch of syrup into the bottom of each jar. Starting from the outside and with the largest slices, arrange the orange slices; place oranges cut-side down against the side of the glass and move to the right, overlapping each orange at its middle section. Working in a circular pattern, pack the jar very tight, until reaching the middle, and twisting the middle piece to form a flower. Hold a butter knife across the top of the oranges to hold down the slices. Top with syrup, leaving ½ inch of headspace.

Remove the air pockets by gently tapping the jar while holding the oranges in place with the knife, top off with syrup to cover the oranges, wipe the rim, and secure the lid. Place the jars in the water bath, covered by 1 inch of water. Once the water is boiling, process for 15 minutes (pages 11–14, steps 7–12).

TIPS

Use wide-mouth half-pints, which will work best for the arrangement.

Use this recipe to make the German Pancake with Orange Syrup (page 76).

Canned

SWEET AND SOUR ORANGE SAUCE

This sauce is inspired by the French dish duck à l'orange, which is traditionally served with oranges or a sauce made with oranges. This version is a bit simpler and less rich, and the long reduction time leads to a tangy, thick, topaz-hued sauce. It is perfect for storing in the cabinet and opening when you have unexpected guests over. This sauce makes it easy to create an impressive meal, because you already put the time in when canning the sauce.

5 medium oranges, divided

¾ cup fresh blood orange juice (from 2 medium blood oranges)

¼ cup fresh lemon juice (from 2 large lemons)

2 cups diced shallots (from about 3 medium bulbs)

3 tablespoons, plus ⅔ cup sherry vinegar, divided

3¼ cups dry white wine (about 1 bottle)

2 tablespoons mustard powder

½ cup granulated sugar

1 ½ teaspoons kosher salt

1 teaspoon annatto powder

Makes 6 quarter-pints

Assemble the canning stations as described on pages 5–7, steps 2–4. At the food preparation station, zest the oranges, saving the zest for the Tomato Skin Togarashi recipe on page 104. Peel 2 of the oranges, saving the peels for the Orange Peel Pickling Spice recipe on page 75. Dice the fruit into 1-inch pieces. Juice the remaining oranges, blood oranges, and lemons. Peel and dice the shallots into 1-inch chunks.

In a medium saucepan over medium heat, sauté the shallots in 3 tablespoons of sherry vinegar until soft, about 5 minutes. Add the remaining ⅔ cup of sherry vinegar, dry white wine, and mustard powder and simmer, whisking until the powder is dissolved; once dissolved, let the sauce reduce for 15 minutes. Add the oranges, orange juice, blood orange juice, and lemon juice and simmer for 15 minutes. Add the sugar, salt, and annatto powder and whisk until dissolved, about 2 minutes.

Place the hot liquid into a blender and blend on low until the orange pieces are small, about 2 minutes. Reduce the sauce another 5 to 10 minutes, until thick and sticky.

At the filling station, keep the jars and sauce hot while filling each jar. Use a heat-resistant pitcher and funnel to pour the sauce into each jar, leaving ½ inch of headspace. Remove the air pockets, wipe the rim, and secure the lid. Place the jars in the water bath, covered by 1 inch of water. Once the water is boiling, process for 10 minutes (pages 11–14, steps 7–12).

TIPS

Annatto powder is made by grinding the seeds of an achiote tree. It can be purchased in specialty grocery stores or online (see Stocking Your Pantry on page 212).

If you can't find annatto, substitute with ¼ teaspoon of ground turmeric and ¼ teaspoon of paprika.

Use this sauce to make the Tea Cup Chicken with Fried Rice on page 75.

Preserved

ORANGE PEEL PICKLING SPICE

This is my ultimate go-to pickling spice. The key here is to use fresh spices and toast them to bring out their flavor. It is perfectly fine to leave the pith (the white part) attached to the orange peel. The more pith you leave, the stronger the bitter note in the pickles, which serves as a nice counterbalance to the sweetness. I love making this recipe to give out as party favors at our canning club meetings or at my pickling classes. I package them in tiny jars for extra cuteness!

1 tablespoon dried orange peels (from 1 orange)

2 tablespoons yellow mustard seeds

1 tablespoon brown mustard seeds

1 tablespoon coriander seeds

½ teaspoon fennel seeds

½ teaspoon dill seeds

1 cinnamon stick

3 dried bay leaves

1½ teaspoons crushed red pepper flakes

6 whole cloves

5 allspice berries

Makes 1 (2-ounce) jar

Preheat the oven to 200°F.

Wash the orange under cold running water and cut off the peel (or use the orange peels reserved from the Sweet and Sour Orange Sauce on page 73). Arrange the orange peels skin-side up on a baking sheet fitted with a silicone baking mat. Place the baking sheet in the center rack of the oven. If you're using a gas oven, leave the door closed. If you're using an electric oven, leave the door propped open to let moisture escape. Flip the orange peels over every 30 minutes, for about 1 to 2 hours. Orange peels should be hard to the touch and dry, while still orange in color. Remove from the oven and let cool.

TIP
Make sure to watch the orange peels closely as they cook. A minute too long will result in browned, burned peels. They need to be dry, but will still be orange in color.

While the orange peels are cooling, toast the mustard seeds, coriander seeds, fennel seeds, and dill seeds over medium heat. Shake the pan every 2 minutes to keep them from burning. After 6 minutes, and when the seeds begin to make popping sounds, remove from the heat and place in a dry bowl.

Crush the cinnamon stick, using a pestle on a wooden cutting board, into ¼-inch (or smaller) pieces. Use kitchen shears to cut the orange peels into ¼-inch pieces. Crumble the bay leaves by hand into the bowl with the seeds. Mix in the remaining spices and orange peels, and place the mixture in a clean bottle. Store in a cool, dry place for up to 6 months.

TIP
Use this pickling spice to make the Pickled Kumquats and Pistachios (page 51).

Recipe

TEA CUP CHICKEN WITH FRIED RICE

This Sichuan-style recipe is traditionally made using equal parts sugar, soy sauce, and rice vinegar, but in this twist we use equal parts Sweet and Sour Orange Sauce (page 73), soy sauce, and sake. It is easy to prepare and super-tasty. Cooking at high temperatures takes a bit of practice, but once you get the hang of it, you will not turn back. If you have a wok, break it out for this dish.

4 whole star anise

¼ cup plus 1 teaspoon soy sauce, divided

1 quarter-pint Sweet and Sour Orange Sauce (page 73)

¼ cup sake

1 teaspoon Sichuan peppercorns

5 tablespoons extra virgin olive oil, divided

2 medium boneless, skinless chicken breasts, cubed

2 shallots, diced

3 medium carrots, sliced

2 celery stalks, sliced

2 cups cooked white rice

1 egg

½ teaspoon kosher salt

1 garlic clove, minced

1 teaspoon curry powder

6 fresh basil leaves, chiffonade

1 scallion, sliced

Makes 2 servings

In a medium bowl, place the star anise, ¼ cup soy sauce, Sweet and

(CONTINUED)

(CONTINUED)
Sour Orange Sauce, and sake. Stir with a spoon and set aside.

In a large, nonstick skillet or wok, toast the peppercorns over medium-high heat until fragrant, shaking the pan every 15 seconds for about 2 minutes. Set the peppercorns on a cutting board and crush under the back of a wooden spoon, then set aside. Place 2 tablespoons of olive oil in the skillet and cook over high heat. Once the oil is hot and fluid, add the cubed chicken. Let it sit, about 3 minutes, so it gets golden brown on one side. Then check one cube and if it has browned, flip over all the chicken cubes so the other side can get brown, about 3 minutes.

Add the shallots and sauté until soft and the liquid is gone. Add the carrots and celery and stir occasionally. Add the crushed peppercorns and the sauce mixture. Bring to a boil over high heat and do not stir; let boil for 2 minutes.

In a large skillet over high heat, place the remaining 3 tablespoons of olive oil. Once the oil is hot, add the rice (it will pop a bit). Move the rice to the sides of the skillet and crack the egg in the center. Sprinkle with salt and garlic and mix into the rice. Turn the heat to medium-high and stir in the curry powder and the remaining 1 teaspoon of soy sauce. Top with some basil.

Serve the chicken over the rice. Garnish with more basil and scallions.

Recipe

GERMAN PANCAKE WITH ORANGE SYRUP

I grew up in a small mountain town called Welches, Oregon, where the key to a day of snow adventures is always a warm breakfast. My favorite such breakfast came from my friend Heidi's mother, Leslie. I don't remember her cooking much, except for something she called "German pancakes"; this recipe is my tribute to her. This version has a lovely nutty sweetness from the orange syrup reduction, and it is the perfect easy breakfast for family members young and old.

1 half-pint Orange Slices in Bergamot Syrup, divided (page 72)

4 tablespoons unsalted butter

¾ cup all-purpose flour

2 tablespoons granulated sugar

¾ cup whole milk

4 large eggs

¼ teaspoon salt

1 teaspoon powdered sugar

Makes 1 large pancake, serves 2

Preheat the oven to 425°F.

Strain the syrup from the orange slices, reserving the slices and 1 tablespoon of the syrup. In a small saucepan over medium heat, reduce the remaining syrup by half, stirring occasionally, about 15 to 20 minutes. Turn off the heat once reduced.

Place a large (12-inch) cast-iron skillet onto the center rack of the oven. Heat until hot, about 5 minutes. Open the oven and add butter to the skillet; let melt, about 3 minutes. Roll the pan around to coat the skillet evenly with butter, also coating the sides with melted butter.

Blend 1 tablespoon bergamot syrup, flour, sugar, milk, eggs, and salt until smooth, about 1 minute. Pour the ingredients into the skillet immediately to ensure that the pancake stays aerated.

Bake until golden-brown and puffed, about 20 to 25 minutes. Serve immediately, before the pancake falls. Top with a dusting of powdered sugar, slices of bergamot oranges, and a drizzle of syrup.

TIP

You can also make this recipe using the Ginger Liqueur Spiked Apples from page 20. Simply substitute 1 teaspoon of almond extract for the 1 tablespoon of bergamot syrup , skip the step of reducing the syrup, and top the pancakes with the apples.

Peaches

One of the great things about having a farmers' market stand is that we are on the front lines of seasonal produce. Two stands down from our booth are our friends at Baird Family Orchards. They grow a variety of stone fruit, such as peaches, plums, apricots, and nectarines. My daughter and I look forward to peach season and are the first buyers of the lovely first-of-the-season Harken peaches, followed by the Fairhavens, and finally the Sunhavens. Packed full of calcium and fiber, the skin of the peach is often peeled and left behind, but I encourage you to eat the skins too so your body can enjoy the vitamin A and vitamin C.

Canned

HABAÑERO GROUND CHERRY PEACH HOT SAUCE

I don't like to use a lot of sugar in my recipes, but when I do it is for a good reason. When canning, the sugar helps the color of the sauce stay nice and bright; without the sugar, it turns brown after a few months. Ground cherries or pineapple tomatillos are fun, hard-to-find ingredients. They appear at the market in late July and are gone by the end of August. That is what makes this sauce so special and why we can make it only once a year. The sauce has a bit of an island feel, but everything is grown right here in Oregon.

3 habañero peppers

¼ cup fresh lemon juice (from about 1 large lemon)

1 pound ground cherries

2 pounds peaches (about 6 medium peaches)

2 cups rice vinegar

¼ cup granulated sugar

1 tablespoon kosher salt

Makes 8 half-pints

Assemble the canning stations as described on pages 5–7, steps 2–4. At the food preparation station, wash the habañeros and remove the stems. Juice the lemon. Pull the husks off the ground cherries and rinse under cold running water. In a large glass bowl, add 4 cups cold water and a few ice cubes and set aside.

Fill a large saucepan half full with water and bring to a boil over high heat. Add the peaches a few at a time and remove with a slotted spoon after 2 minutes. Put the peaches into the bowl of cold water. Once the peaches are cool to the touch, remove the peels and the stones by hand, saving for the Peach Stone Tonic recipe on page 81.

Dump the water out of the pot. Add the peaches, ground cherries, habañeros, rice vinegar, and lemon juice, and cook over medium heat. Once the contents are bubbling, cook uncovered for 10 minutes, stirring occasionally to avoid sticking. Add the sugar and salt, and stir to combine.

Blend in the blender on high for 3 minutes, until no seeds are visible. Let the blender sit for 5 minutes to reduce the froth produced from blending.

At the filling station, keep the jars and sauce hot while filling each jar. Pour directly from the blender and fill each jar with sauce, leaving ½ inch of headspace. Tap the jars gently and remove the air pockets, stirring with a chopstick, then let sit for 2 minutes. Wipe the rim and secure the lid. Place the jars in the water bath, covered by 1 inch of water. Once the water is boiling, process for 10 minutes (pages 11–14, steps 7–12).

TIP

Use this recipe to make the Habañero Meatballs with Cauliflower Rice (page 83).

Canned

PEACH AND LAVENDER JAM

Making this jam is a beloved summer tradition in my family. We drive out to an orchard for the day, pick dozens of peaches, and gather lavender. Each time I open this jar, I think about our fun day at the farm. The jam turns out smooth and fragrant and is perfect for slathering on toast or glazing grilled meats. My friend Miranda Rake inspired this recipe; she has an outstanding artisanal jam business called Plum Tree Jams. My favorite thing about her jams is that she keeps them simple so she can showcase the fruit.

4 pounds peaches (from about 12 peaches)

½ cup fresh lemon juice (from 2 large lemons)

2 cups granulated sugar

1⅓ cups Lavender Pear Peel Pectin (page 87)

Makes 7 half-pints

Assemble the canning stations as described on pages 5–7, steps 2–4. At the food preparation station, wash the peaches. Cut the peaches into 2-inch chunks, remove the stones, and set the stones aside for the Peach Stone Tonic recipe on opposite page.

In a large, shallow, heavy-bottom skillet, place all the ingredients. Bring the pot to a boil over high heat; once bubbling, turn the heat down to medium. Stir and let simmer, uncovered, for 30 minutes.

Blend with an immersion blender until smooth. Turn the heat to a low simmer and let cook uncovered for 10 more minutes, stirring while waiting for the mixture to reach the desired thickness.

At the filling station, keep the jars and jam hot while filling each jar. Use a funnel and ladle to fill each jar with jam, leaving ¼ inch of headspace. Remove the air pockets, wipe the rims, and secure the lids. Place the jars in the water bath, covered by 1 inch of water. Once the water is boiling, process for 10 minutes (pages 11–14, steps 7–12).

TIP

If you did not make the Lavender Pear Peel Pectin, you can purchase store-bought pectin. Follow the instructions on the package for making peach jam using four pounds of fruit.

Preserved

PEACH STONE TONIC

My husband loves gin and tonics, so we always keep a bottle of this tonic syrup on hand in our fridge to easily assemble his favorite nightcap. Use the tonic syrup in a 1:3 ratio (1 part tonic: 3 parts sparkling water). This version has the classic bitter element from the cinchona bark, the tangy balance from the citric acid and citrus peels, and is rounded out by a bit of spice.

1 orange

1 grapefruit

2 stalks lemongrass

6 peach stones (reserved from Peach and Lavender Jam, opposite page)

3 tablespoons cinchona bark

1 tablespoon citric acid

1 teaspoon salt

10 black peppercorns

3 whole star anise

¼ teaspoon dried allspice berries

½ cup local honey

Makes 6 quarter-pints

At the preparation station, wash the citrus under cold running water. Using a sharp paring knife, cut the citrus peel off the orange and grapefruit and slice the peel into strips. Cut the orange and grapefruit in half and juice. Slice the lemongrass into ½-inch chunks and cut off the root end and any brown pieces.

In a medium, stainless steel saucepan, place 3 cups of water, citrus peels, citrus juice, peach stones, cinchona bark, citric acid, salt, peppercorns, star anise, and allspice berries. Bring to a boil over high heat; once boiling, turn to a low simmer. Let simmer, uncovered, for 20 minutes.

Strain the liquid through a fine-mesh strainer, catching the liquid in a bowl. Pour the liquid through a coffee filter or jelly bag to get out any tiny particles. Rinse the pot and place the double-strained liquid back into the clean pot. Over medium heat, stir in the honey, turn the heat to low, and let simmer for 10 minutes.

Pour into a sterilized bottle and store in the refrigerator for up to 3 months.

CAUTION

Be very careful when working with barks and roots. Follow the specified amount and use pieces of bark instead of powders, in order to strain the bark out. It is not recommended to consume cinchona bark if you're pregnant or breast-feeding.

TIP

You can purchase cinchona bark and citric acid from organic herb and spice retailers (see Stocking Your Pantry on page 212).

Recipe

HABAÑERO MEATBALLS WITH CAULIFLOWER RICE

Don't be scared off by the habañero—this dish is palatable to all. The beautiful floral aromatics of the peppers are highlighted, while the coconut milk lessens the kick. The sauce is interwoven with the cauliflower rice and meatballs, with textural elements from the sprouts and almonds. It is both comforting and unusual and makes a perfect warm winter lunch. We often put chicken breast in the food processor to make meatballs, meat loaf, and chicken tacos. The result is a low-fat, high-protein alternative to using ground beef.

Olive oil cooking spray

1 head white cauliflower

1 tablespoon olive oil

1 pound boneless, skinless chicken breasts

2 cups coconut milk, divided

½ cup panko breadcrumbs, divided

1 green apple, diced

2 tablespoons fresh lime juice

1 medium egg

½ teaspoon dried basil

½ teaspoon oregano

¼ teaspoon crushed red pepper flakes

½ teaspoon kosher salt

⅛ teaspoon fresh ground pepper

¼ cup Liquid Gold Vegetable Stock (page 52)

½ cup Habañero Ground Cherry Peach Hot Sauce (page 79)

½ teaspoon curry powder

¼ cup toasted almonds

½ cup alfalfa sprouts

1 hot red pepper, sliced

Makes 2 servings

Spray the inside of a food processor with olive oil cooking spray. Break the cauliflower into medium-sized florets. Put half the florets into the mixer and pulse 6 to 10 times, until rice-sized. Pour into a large bowl and repeat with the second half.

In a large skillet, place 1 tablespoon of olive oil and heat over medium-high heat, until shimmery. Add the cauliflower, sauté for 2 minutes, and cover and cook for 5 minutes. Move cauliflower to a plate to cool.

Roughly cube the chicken breasts and place in the food processor. Pulse 15 to 20 times until evenly ground.

Put ¼ cup of coconut milk into a large mixing bowl and add ¼ cup of panko breadcrumbs, mix. Let sit for 10 minutes.

Dice the apple into ¼-inch cubes and toss with the lime juice. Set aside.

Preheat the oven to 350°F. Line a large baking sheet with parchment paper.

In the large mixing bowl containing the breadcrumb mixture, add the chicken, egg, basil, oregano, crushed red pepper flakes, salt, pepper, and the remaining ¼ cup of breadcrumbs; mix by hand until combined. Shape into 1-inch meatballs. Place the meatballs onto the baking sheet, about ½ inch apart. Bake for 20 to 30 minutes.

While the meatballs are cooking, heat the remaining 1¾ cups of coconut milk in a large skillet over medium heat, until warm. Stir in the Liquid Gold Vegetable Stock, Habañero Ground Cherry Peach Hot Sauce, and curry powder. Turn to a low simmer and whisk for a couple minutes until the curry powder has dissolved.

Remove the meatballs from the oven once they're golden brown and cooked through. Place the meatballs into the saucepan and coat with the sauce.

Plate in individual shallow bowls. Place the cauliflower rice in the bottom of the bowl, add the meatballs, and cover with sauce. Top with the apple, almonds, alfalfa sprouts, and hot red pepper.

Pears

Oregonians love pears and are one of the top producers of this beautiful fruit. We even hold annual pear blossom festivals to celebrate Oregon's epic pear production. The celebration honors the farmers who grow and care for these fragile harvests, as it takes much coddling to get perfect pear specimens. Pears contain more fiber than most fruits and much of that is found in the skins. Unfortunately, the antioxidant-rich peels are often discarded. This chapter highlights the pectin stored in these wonderful fruits and skins, which is great for jams and jellies. The pear is a true full-use fruit.

Sparkling Wine Poached Pears, page 86.

Canned

SPARKLING WINE POACHED PEARS

Simmered in a high-quality sparkling wine, these festive pears are definitely an adult treat. They are a favorite of my father-in-law's, who enjoys them over ice cream or paired with goat cheese, as they are in the Pear Galette with Goat Cheese (page 89). I use D'Anjou pears here because I can find them at the farmers' market almost all year round, but you can substitute any firm pear you have on hand. (See photo page 85.)

½ cup plus 2 tablespoons fresh lemon juice, divided

9 large D'Anjou pears

3¼ cups (1 bottle) dry sparkling wine

10 sprigs fresh thyme, divided

½ cup Vanilla Bean Lemonade (page 56)

½ cup granulated sugar

4 small dried bay leaves

5 whole peppercorns

Makes 6 pints

Assemble the canning stations as described on pages 5–7, steps 2–4. At the preparation station, juice the lemon. Place 2 tablespoons of the lemon juice into a large bowl of water. Wash the pears and peel the skins. Set the skins aside for the Lavender Pear Peel Pectin recipe on opposite page. Slice the pears lengthwise from stem to base in whole ¼-inch-thick slices, popping out any visible seeds and trimming the blossom end. Place the pears into the bowl of lemon water to keep them from browning.

In a large, heavy-bottom saucepan over medium heat, add the sparkling wine, ½ cup of lemon juice, 4 sprigs thyme, Vanilla Bean Lemonade, sugar, bay leaves, and peppercorns. Then turn the heat to the lowest setting, stirring occasionally for 3 minutes, until the sugar is dissolved.

At the filling station, keep the jars and syrup hot while filling each. Starting with the large slices, pack cold pears into the jars, bottom-side down, and filling in the gaps with small pieces. Slide a thyme sprig into each jar along the glass to ensure visibility. Use a funnel and a heat-resistant pitcher to cover the pears with syrup, leaving ½ inch of headspace. Remove the air pockets, wipe the rims, and secure the lids. Place the jars in the water bath, covered by 1 inch of water. Once the water is boiling, process for 15 minutes (pages 11–14, steps 7–12).

TIPS

If you did not make the Vanilla Bean Lemonade, substitute with pineapple juice, not from concentrate.

Use wide-mouth pint jars to get the large slices in without breaking them.

Use these pears to make the Pear Galette with Goat Cheese (page 89).

Canned

PEAR AND THYME RELISH

This condiment in the South is often called chow-chow and is made up of whatever kitchen scraps need a home. Cabbage, peppers, onions, and tomatillos make up the usual relish, but my recipe includes a northwestern twist, with pears replacing the tomatillos and cabbage. It is a wonderful recipe to make in the fall, and you can use any type of pear you find or have on hand. We have a Bartlett pear tree in our yard, which is what I often like to use.

6 ripe pears (about 4 cups prepped)

2 green bell peppers

1 medium yellow onion

¼ cup fresh lemon juice (from about 1 lemon)

3 stalks celery

2½ cups distilled vinegar, divided

2 tablespoons kosher salt

1 tablespoon brown mustard seeds

1 teaspoon dried thyme

½ teaspoon crushed red pepper flakes

½ teaspoon ground turmeric

¼ cup light brown sugar

Makes 6 half-pints

Assemble the canning stations as described on pages 5–7, steps 2–4. Wash the pears; peel and core them and cut them into 2-inch chunks, saving the peels and cores for the Lavender Pear Peel Pectin recipe at right. Wash the bell peppers, cut out the stems and remove the seeds, and cut into ½-inch cubes. Peel the onion and cut into 1-inch cubes. Juice the lemon. Wash the celery and cut into ½-inch pieces.

In a large, nonreactive pot, place 1 cup of water, 1 cup of vinegar, pears, bell peppers, onion, celery, lemon juice, salt, mustard seeds, thyme, crushed red pepper flakes, and turmeric. Bring to a boil over high heat. Once boiling, turn the heat down to a low simmer and cook for 30 minutes, until all the liquid is gone, but before the vegetables stick to the bottom of the pot. Add the remaining 1½ cups of vinegar, 1½ cups of water, and brown sugar and stir in the pot. Simmer uncovered for 10 minutes, stirring occasionally. Break apart any large pieces of pear with a wooden spoon.

At the filling station, keep the jars and relish hot while filling each jar. Ladle the contents into a heat-resistant pitcher and use a funnel to fill each jar, leaving ½ inch of headspace. Remove the air pockets, wipe the rim, and secure the lid. Place the jars in the water bath, covered by 1 inch of water. Once the water is boiling, process for 10 minutes (pages 11–14, steps 7–12).

Preserved

LAVENDER PEAR PEEL PECTIN

This pectin is used specifically to make the Peach and Lavender Jam on page 80. While it can't be subbed in for every pectin recipe, it is a really nice fit for that recipe. In this application the pectin comes from the peels and cores of our fruit friend the pear. The acidity from the lemon brightens the flavor and keeps the pectin from browning, and the lavender elevates the saved fruit with a hint of aromatics.

6 pear peels and cores (reserved from Pear and Thyme Relish, left)

¼ cup fresh lemon juice (from about 1 lemon)

1 tablespoon dried lavender

Makes 3 cups

Place all the ingredients and 4 cups of water in a medium, nonreactive saucepan and bring to a boil over high heat. Once boiling, reduce the heat to a medium-low simmer and cook uncovered for 30 minutes. Check on the mixture occasionally and turn the heat down if it's bubbling rapidly or if the pears are sticking to the bottom of the pot.

Strain the mixture through a fine-mesh strainer, pressing out any liquid from the skins and cores, compost the remaining pulp. Store in the refrigerator for up to 5 days or use immediately.

TIP

Use this pectin to make the Peach and Lavender Jam (page 80).

Recipe

PEAR GALETTE WITH GOAT CHEESE

We share our commercial kitchen space with Portland Creamery, and they make the most luxurious soft and creamy goat cheeses. When we co-host events, this is an impressive galette to stun our guests with and we often dollop it with the Habañero Ground Cherry Peach Hot Sauce (page 79). The simple pear shape takes very few pastry skills, but is sure to impress.

½ cup salted butter

1¼ cups (plus some for rolling) unbleached all-purpose flour

½ teaspoon kosher salt

2 pint jars Sparkling Wine Poached Pears (page 86)

3 sprigs fresh thyme

6 ounces soft goat cheese

1 egg

Makes 1 galette

Cut the butter into ½-inch cubes and place in the freezer; remove after 15 minutes. Place ¼ cup of water and 3 ice cubes into a medium bowl. Set aside.

In a large bowl, place the flour, salt, and cold butter. Cut the ingredients together with a pastry cutter or 2 butter knives.

When all the dough is pea-sized, drizzle 1 tablespoon of cold water from the water bowl around the edge of the bowl and work it in with a fork. Keep adding water 1 tablespoon at a time until the pastry holds together without crumbling; it will take about 5 to 6 tablespoons in all. Form the dough into a ball, wrap with plastic wrap, and chill in the refrigerator for 1 hour.

Line a baking sheet with parchment paper. Drain the pears, saving the liquid for later cocktails or sparkling water. Remove the thyme leaves from the stems.

Take the pie dough out of the refrigerator. Place the ball of dough on a lightly floured surface and flour the rolling pin. Flatten the ball and roll the dough out from the center, making a circle; when it gets to be 6 inches in diameter, begin shaping the dough into an oval by pressing the rolling pin up and out. Continue adding flour if needed to keep the dough from sticking. Roll the bottom wider in diameter while keeping the top oblong. Manipulate it by hand into a pear shape. Slide it onto the parchment-lined baking sheet.

Place quarter-sized drops of goat cheese randomly across the surface, leaving a 1-inch border of dough. Find the best-looking whole pear with the stem attached, and place it on the top center with the stem protruding from the top of the dough. Begin overlapping slices of pear, with slices fanning slightly outward from the center. Maintain the 1-inch border.

Starting at the bottom of the tart, begin pleating the dough and folding it over to the left every inch until you reach the top. Whisk the egg with a splash of cold water and paint the exposed crust with a pastry brush.

Bake until the edges are golden and crisp to the touch, about 1 hour. Remove from the oven and sprinkle with the thyme leaves.

TIP
If you did not make the Sparkling Wine Poached Pears, you can substitute with fresh pears tossed in lemon juice and sprinkled with thyme.

Plums

Portland streets are lined with fruit trees, so our neighborhood holds a harvest swap. Anything not claimed at the swap is donated to Apples-to-Applesauce, a local nonprofit with a goal of ending hunger by preserving food that would normally go to waste. Katrina, the founder, makes food for schools and group homes (the same programs I used to work for) from donated food collected by volunteers. This swap also kicks off our plum experiments with sauces, jams, jellies, and especially chutneys. All varieties of plums are packed full of vitamins, fiber, and minerals that promote digestive health. There are so many plum varieties, but my favorite is the Italian plum, which has the fascinating ability to start with green flesh and then turn red when cooked.

Canned

CRANBERRY PLUM SAUCE

My friend's mother introduced me to the spice blend for this sauce. She speaks very little English and I speak zero Russian, but we always communicate with love and joy. One day she invited us over for lunch, and we feasted on pickled goodies, cured meats, and soft cheeses. I couldn't get enough of the pickled carrots that were made with her special spices. She sent me home with my own bag of Khmeli-Suneli, a Georgian spice blend. I have included my recipe for this delicious blend, which has been Grandma-approved (after she told me it needed more coriander!). The spice blend works nicely with plums and this sauce is perfect for dredging over slices of slow-roasted pork loin. It is tart, sweet, and spicy, bringing a tasty party to your mouth.

2 pounds red plums (about 14 medium plums)

2 red bell peppers

2 garlic cloves

½ cup unsweetened cranberry juice

½ cup red wine vinegar

2 tablespoons Khmeli-Suneli Georgian Spice Blend (right)

1 tablespoon light brown sugar

1 tablespoon kosher salt

½ teaspoon cayenne pepper

Makes 6 half-pints

Assemble the canning stations as described on pages 5–7, steps 2–4. At the food preparation station, wash the plums and cut into quarters; remove the stones and save them for the Hibiscus Plum Shrub on page 94. Wash the peppers and remove the stems and seeds; roughly chop the peppers. Peel and dice the garlic.

In a large saucepan, place all the ingredients and bring to a boil over high heat. Once at a boil, turn the heat down to medium and simmer, uncovered, for 20 minutes, stirring occasionally to avoid sticking.

Blend the contents of the pot in a blender until smooth; blend on high for 4 to 6 minutes, until there are no visible skins. Let the mixture sit in the blender for 5 minutes.

At the filling station, keep the jars and sauce hot while filling each jar. Use a funnel to pour the sauce directly into the jar, leaving ½ inch of headspace. Remove the air pockets, wipe the rim, and secure the lid. Place the jars in the water bath, covered by 1 inch of water. Once the water is boiling, process for 10 minutes (pages 11–14, steps 7–12).

TIPS

To find out more about unsweetened cranberry juice, see Stocking Your Pantry (page 212).

Use this sauce to make the Fried Chicken Wings with Plum Sauce (page 97).

KHMELI-SUNELI GEORGIAN SPICE BLEND

2 teaspoons coriander

1 teaspoon kosher salt

1 teaspoon fenugreek seeds

1 teaspoon sweet paprika

1 teaspoon marjoram

1 bay leaf, crushed

½ teaspoon dried basil

½ teaspoon marigold petals

½ teaspoon celery seed

½ teaspoon parsley

½ teaspoon dill

½ teaspoon mint

½ teaspoon ground turmeric

Makes 3 tablespoons

Grind all the spices in a mortar and pestle or spice grinder until powdered.

TIP

You can also use the Khmeli-Suneli to make the Golden Pickled Beets (page 120).

Canned

SPICED PLUM CHUTNEY

My aunt Pammy loved apricots and every year she would request an apricot pie for her birthday. From the moment I learned these stone fruits were her favorite, every time I see them fresh or dried, I think of her. The Italian plums I use here have a purple skin with yellow flesh and roll into our markets in late August. The warming spices in the Garam Masala Spice Blend make this sweet, sticky, and savory chutney—it's the perfect addition to any cheese board.

3 pounds Italian plums (about 20 medium plums)

3 cups dried apricots

1½ cups malt vinegar

2 tablespoons Garam Masala Spice Blend (right)

1 cup light brown sugar, loosely packed

1 tablespoon kosher salt

Makes 6 pints

Assemble the canning stations as described on pages 5–7, steps 2–4. At the food preparation station, wash the plums under cold running water. Remove the stones and roughly dice the plums; save the stones for the Hibiscus Plum Shrub recipe on page 94. Roughly dice the apricots.

In a large, nonreactive skillet, place ½ cup of water and all the ingredients and bring to a boil over high heat. Once hot and bubbly, turn the heat down to a simmer and cook uncovered for 45 minutes, stirring occasionally, until thick.

At the filling station, keep the jars and chutney hot while filling each jar. Use a funnel and a ladle to fill each jar, leaving ½ inch of headspace. Remove the air pockets, wipe the rim, and secure the lid. Place the jars in the water bath, covered by 1 inch of water. Once the water is boiling, process for 10 minutes (pages 11–14, steps 7–12).

TIP

While you can purchase garam masala in specialty grocery stores, you can also make your own! See recipe at right.

GARAM MASALA SPICE BLEND

1 tablespoon cumin seeds

1 teaspoon coriander

1 teaspoon black peppercorns

½ teaspoon freshly grated nutmeg

½ teaspoon crushed red pepper flakes

¼ teaspoon cardamom seeds

4 cloves

2 bay leaves

1-inch piece cinnamon stick

Makes 2 tablespoons

Grind all the spices with a mortar and pestle or in a spice grinder until powdered.

Preserved

HIBISCUS PLUM SHRUB

A shrub is a fruit-based, infused vinegar that can be added to cocktails, but my favorite use is as an ingredient in salad dressing. Feel free to substitute another type of fruit as well, since you are not canning it. This recipe is a tangy, exciting way to enjoy seasonal fruit flavors throughout the year and is a great way to use fruit that is not so pretty. It calls for coconut vinegar, which makes the shrub a bit more like a Japanese drinking vinegar, perfect for mixing with sparking wine; mix 1 part shrub to 5 parts bubbles.

2 red plums

10 plum stones (reserved from Cranberry Plum Sauce, page 91)

½ cup granulated sugar

2 cups coconut vinegar

1 tablespoon dried hibiscus petals

Makes 2 cups

At the preparation station, cut the plums from the stones and dice the flesh into 1-inch chunks. Place in a bowl with the reserved stones and the sugar and mash the fruit with a fork. Let the fruit sit for 15 minutes, stirring occasionally.

Heat the coconut vinegar and dried hibiscus petals in a medium saucepan over high heat, stirring occasionally, until boiling, about 4 minutes. Once boiling, reduce the heat to medium; add the fruit and sugar and let simmer for 5 minutes, stirring occasionally to avoid sticking. Turn off the heat and let the liquid infuse for 10 minutes.

Once the liquid has infused, strain through a coffee filter, compost any remaining pulp and stones. Pour the strained shrub into a sterilized glass bottle. Label the jar and store in the refrigerator for up to 6 months.

TIPS

If you do not have extra plum stones, you can make the shrub with four whole plums instead.

Use this shrub to make the Fried Chicken Wings with Plum Sauce (page 97).

Recipe

FRIED CHICKEN WINGS WITH PLUM SAUCE

I make fried chicken once a year for my family on Easter—my brother Dave loves it. Soaking it in buttermilk overnight is great if you have the time, but if it's last minute, a vinegar braise with high heat is your savior. It maintains the moisture without drying out the meat while frying at a high temperature. Once the chicken is out of the fryer, the sauce creates a beautiful lacquer over your crispy wings.

1 cup Hibiscus Plum Shrub (page 94)

1½ cups distilled vinegar

1 tablespoon plus 1 teaspoon kosher salt, divided

2 pounds small chicken wings and/or drumsticks

4 cups vegetable oil

1 ½ cups buttermilk

1 cup all-purpose flour

1 teaspoon baking powder

¼ teaspoon ground black pepper

¼ teaspoon cayenne pepper

1 half-pint Cranberry Plum Sauce (page 91)

Makes 16 wings

Create a poaching liquid by combining the Hibiscus Plum Shrub, distilled vinegar, and 1 tablespoon of salt. In a medium saucepan fitted with a lid, bring the poaching liquid to a boil over high heat. Once boiling, add the chicken to the liquid, making sure the wings are covered with liquid, and turn the heat to a low simmer. Cover the pot and let it simmer for 20 minutes. Move the chicken to a kitchen towel-lined plate, pat dry, and let cool.

In a large, deep, cast-iron skillet, heat the vegetable oil over high heat. (Note: The pan should be a little under halfway filled with oil so as not to have any spillover.) Allow the oil to reach 325°F and check with a high temperature thermometer.

Line a baking sheet with a brown paper bag and top with a wire cooling rack. Set aside.

While the oil is heating and the chicken is cooling, create the dredging station by pouring the buttermilk into a medium bowl. In a separate medium bowl, whisk together the flour, the remaining 1 teaspoon of salt, baking powder, black pepper, and cayenne pepper. Wearing gloves, dip each chicken wing into the buttermilk and then shake off any extra liquid. Evenly coat the chicken in the flour mixture. Place onto a clean dry plate.

Fry the chicken in the oil, turning every minute with tongs, until golden and crunchy, about 2 to 6 minutes. Transfer the chicken to the cooling rack. Using a pastry brush, coat each piece with the Cranberry Plum Sauce.

TIPS

If you did not make the Hibiscus Plum Shrub, use another shrub or replace it with distilled vinegar.

If you did not make the Cranberry Plum Sauce, replace it with your favorite vinegar-based wing sauce.

Red Tomatoes

Of all the beautiful bounty of produce, there is one priceless gem that stands above all others for me, and that jewel is a fresh, in-season, outdoor-grown tomato. There is a very small window for Portlanders to get our hands on these pure, juicy red tomatoes. During this three-month run, I can about 3,000 pounds of tomatoes to use in our sauces during the winter—this is the true heart of our recipes. Tomato season starts with colorful, sweet cherry tomatoes, moving into Early Girls, Romas, and finally heirlooms. All contain lycopene, which is a powerful antioxidant in the tomato skins. This chapter walks you through drying and powdering the skins, which can then be used in many ways for later consumption—dried tomato skin powder is a great thickening agent for sauces.

Canned

ROASTED SUMMER SAVORY TOMATOES

Savory is an herb that grows in two seasons—there is a summer savory and a winter savory. I prefer summer savory because it is less bitter and a bit sweet, with a flavor comparable to thyme. My savory plant is in full bloom at the same time that my tomatoes are popping. Adding in the sprigs of savory creates a flavor that is mild enough to let us use these tomatoes in any recipe calling for canned tomatoes throughout the year, such as sauces, salsas, and soups. Tomatoes of the heirloom variety are less acidic and need a bit of citric acid to be safe for water bath canning.

10 pounds heirloom tomatoes (about 25 large tomatoes)

8 sprigs summer savory

2 tablespoons kosher salt

1 tablespoon plus 1½ teaspoons citric acid, divided

Makes 6 pints

TIP
If you don't want to use summer savory, you can substitute with your favorite fresh herbs.

Preheat the oven to 500°F.

Assemble the canning stations as described on pages 5–7, steps 2–4. At the food preparation station, wash the tomatoes and slice in half widthwise. Line 2 baking sheets with parchment paper and lay the tomatoes cut-side up on the trays. Wash the savory and trim to fit inside the pint jars, leaving 1 inch from the top.

Place the baking sheets in the oven. Roast the tomatoes for 15 to 18 minutes, until the sides of the skin appear wrinkled. Remove the baking sheets and let the tomatoes cool for 15 minutes. Once cool enough to handle safely, peel off the skins over a large pot; hand-crushing the tomatoes, pull out any hard cores or stems. Squeeze all pulp from the skin and save for the Tomato Skin Togarashi recipe on page 104. In a large pot over medium-high heat, place the salt, 1 tablespoon of citric acid, and tomatoes and stir. Bring the tomatoes to a boil; once bubbling, turn the heat to the lowest setting.

At the filling station, keep the jars and tomatoes hot. Place ¼ teaspoon of citric acid into each jar. Use a funnel and a heat-resistant pitcher to fill the jar halfway and place a summer savory sprig against the jar wall to ensure it's visible. Fill with tomatoes, leaving ½ inch of headspace. Remove the air pockets, wipe the rim, and secure the lid. Place the jars in the water bath, covered by 1 inch of water. Once the water is boiling, process for 15 minutes (pages 11–14, steps 7–12).

TIP
I use a gas oven, which does not have a broiler or a broil setting. If you have an electric oven, set it to the highest temperature, without broiling. You do not want the tops to brown; you are simply looking to hit the tomatoes with high heat so you can easily remove the skins.

Canned

WHITE WINE MARINARA SAUCE

Many of our sauces rely on heirloom salad tomatoes of Czechoslovakian origin, called Stupice (pronounced stoo-PEECH-ka). Tomatoes have a short growing season here in the Pacific Northwest, but these beauties thrive in our climate. Plus, the skins are soft and there is no core, making for easy prep. This recipe requires a blender that can liquefy the tomato skins and seeds. The sauce has a long reducing time, but when you are enjoying this summery sauce in the winter, the time you put in is so worth it!

6 pounds heirloom salad tomatoes (about 60 small tomatoes)

8 celery stalks (about 2 cups prepped)

2 medium onions (about 3 cups prepped)

10 garlic cloves

1 cup white balsamic vinegar, divided

2 cups dry white wine

2 tablespoons kosher salt, plus more to taste

2 tablespoon dried basil

1 tablespoon dried marjoram

1 tablespoon dried thyme

1 teaspoon crushed red pepper flakes

Makes 6 pints

Assemble the canning stations as described on pages 5–7, steps 2–4. At the food preparation station, wash the tomatoes and compost the stems. Working in batches, place half of the tomatoes into the blender and pulse until no skins and seeds are visible, about 5 minutes. Place the tomatoes into a bowl and repeat the process with the remaining tomatoes. Wash the celery and cut into ¼-inch pieces. Peel the onions and cut them into ¼-inch cubes. Peel the garlic and roughly mince.

Heat ½ cup of vinegar in a large, nonreactive, heavy-bottom saucepan over medium-high heat. Once the vinegar is hot, add the onions, garlic, and celery and sauté, stirring occasionally, for 5 minutes, until the onion is tender. Add the white wine, the remaining ½ cup of vinegar, salt, herbs and spices. Let cook for 3 minutes, until fragrant. Add the tomatoes, turn the heat up to high, and bring to a boil. Once the contents are bubbling, reduce the heat to a low simmer. Let simmer uncovered for 1 hour and 45 minutes, stirring occasionally. Lower the heat as the sauce reduces; the sauce should be bubbling but not splattering. Add salt to taste.

At the filling station, keep the jars and sauce hot while filling each jar. Use a heat-resistant pitcher and funnel to fill each jar with sauce, leaving ½ inch of headspace. Remove the air pockets by tapping the jar gently on a kitchen towel. Wipe the rim and secure the lid. Place the jars in the water bath, covered by 1 inch of water. Once the water is boiling, process for 10 minutes (pages 11–14, steps 7–12).

TIP

Use this sauce to make the Tomato Bisque with Crab (page 104).

MASON

Canned

PURPLE BASIL PICKLED CHERRY TOMATOES

Keeping pickled goods from floating is an age-old problem. We tested many theories—piercing each tomato with a pin was the most time-consuming, but keeps the skins from splitting. We found that the champion practice is to weigh down particularly buoyant items with a slice of citrus. It adds a touch of acid while also fixing your floating problem. I like to can these pickled tomatoes in glass-lid jars to show off the citrus topper. These jars are simply stunning, with beautiful herbs, purple brine, and glowing cherry tomatoes.

6½ cups mixed cherry tomatoes
½ cup purple basil
8 fresh bay leaves, divided
8 sprigs fresh thyme, divided
2 sprigs fresh oregano
2 large limes
6 garlic cloves
4 cups rice vinegar
2 tablespoons salt
¼ teaspoon pink peppercorns
Makes 6 pints

Assemble the canning stations as described on pages 5–7, steps 2–4. Wash the tomatoes and the fresh herbs under cold running water. Remove any green stems from the tomatoes. Leaving the peels on, slice the limes into ¼-inch-thick rounds and set aside for the filling station. Peel the garlic cloves.

In a medium, heavy-bottom saucepan, place the vinegar, 3 cups of water, salt, peppercorns, purple basil, 2 bay leaves, 2 sprigs of thyme, and the sprigs of oregano. Bring to a boil over high heat. Once boiling, turn the heat to a low simmer and let steep for 5 minutes. Drain the brine through a fine-mesh strainer into a heat-resistant pitcher.

At the filling station, keep the jars and brine hot while filling each jar. Place a garlic clove in the bottom and fill the jar halfway with tomatoes. Place a bay leaf against the glass, ensuring visibility. Place a sprig of thyme on the opposite side against the glass. Fill the jar the rest of the way with tomatoes, leaving 1 inch of headspace. Place a lime slice on top and hold it with a chopstick. Top with the brine, leaving ½ inch of headspace. Remove the air pockets, wipe the rim, and secure the lid. Place the jars in the water bath, covered by 1 inch of water. Once the water is boiling, process for 10 minutes (pages 11–14, steps 7–12).

TIPS

Using purple basil gives the brine a lovely pink hue, but you can use any basil you have on hand.

Use these tomatoes to make the Oven-Roasted Chicken Thighs with Pickled Tomatoes (page 107).

Preserved

TOMATO SKIN TOGARASHI

Togarashi—a Japanese blend traditionally made up of seven spices—is most commonly seen in ramen shops and is salty, spicy, earthy, and tangy. Fair warning: This recipe involves roasting, toasting, and drying. Timing is key, as things can quickly burn or brown, so you have to watch each baking sheet with a close eye. The work is worth the time, however, as this spice blend is great for your homemade ramen bowl and also makes the perfect avocado topper for a quick, simple, healthy snack.

3 tomato skins (1 tablespoon ground) (reserved from Roasted Summer Savory Tomatoes page 100)

2 tablespoons orange zest (from about 3 oranges) (reserved from the Turmeric Ginger Juice Shots, page 189)

1 tablespoon white sesame seeds

1 tablespoon black sesame seeds

1 teaspoon dried seaweed (I like wakame seaweed for this)

½ teaspoon crushed red pepper flakes

¼ teaspoon black peppercorns

Makes ¼ cup

Preheat the oven to 200°F. Line 2 baking sheets with parchment paper.

Spread the skins onto one baking sheet. Place on the bottom rack of the oven and set the timer for 30 minutes. After 30 minutes, flip the tomato skins and return to the oven for 15 minutes. The tomato skins are done when they are still red but completely dry.

While the skins are drying, use a box grater to zest 3 oranges. Evenly sprinkle the orange zest onto the second baking sheet. Place the sheet on the top rack of the oven and cook for 8 minutes. Remove the sheet from the oven and crush the orange zest between 2 fingers. Return the sheet to the oven for 10 minutes. Take it out again and crumble the zest between your fingers. Return to the oven for 15 minutes. The orange zest is done when it's still orange but completely dry.

While the skins and peels are drying, toast the sesame seeds over medium-low heat in a small, dry skillet. Cook for about 2 minutes, shaking every 15 seconds. When golden, quickly move the seeds to a plate to cool.

Once completely dry and cool, use a mortar and pestle or a spice grinder to grind the tomato skins into a fine powder. Place in a medium bowl. Grind the seaweed, crushed red pepper flakes, and black peppercorns until fine and add to the bowl. Mix in the orange zest and sesame seeds. Store in an airtight jar out of direct sunlight for up to 6 months.

TIP

If you did not make the marinara sauce or vegetable stock, replace them with your favorite sauce and stock.

Recipe

TOMATO BISQUE WITH CRAB

This soup is your reward for the lengthy time it took to make the White Wine Marinara Sauce! While technically not bisque, it could easily become bisque by making seafood stock out of the crab shells. The creamy coconut milk softens the flavorful marinara sauce, making it a perfect complement to the crab, and the fish sauce adds a lovely umami finish. This is a quick, easy, and impressive soup.

1 pint White Wine Marinara Sauce (page 101)

1 pint Liquid Gold Vegetable Stock (page 52)

1 can (13½ ounces) coconut milk

1 teaspoon fish sauce

1 teaspoon kosher salt

1 tablespoon fresh lime juice (from about 1 lime)

½ pound lump crabmeat

2 scallions, thinly sliced

Makes 2 servings

Heat the marinara sauce, vegetable stock, and coconut milk in a large saucepan over medium heat, stirring occasionally until bubbly, about 6 minutes. Reduce the heat to a simmer and add the fish sauce and salt. Let simmer uncovered for 10 minutes, stirring occasionally.

Turn the heat off and stir in the lime juice. Pour the soup into 2 bowls and top with the crabmeat and scallions.

Recipe

OVEN-ROASTED CHICKEN THIGHS WITH PICKLED TOMATOES

Perfect for a weeknight dinner, this Tuscan-inspired recipe is easy to prep and full of flavor. The pickled tomato pairs well with the salty olives and capers, and brings a note of summer to this cold-weather meal. The chicken skin gets crisp and golden without an additional step of browning.

1 medium celery stalk

1 medium carrot

2 garlic cloves

2 small shallots

1 large lemon

2 sprigs fresh thyme

2 sprigs fresh oregano

2 bay leaves

4 chicken thighs, bone in and skin on

½ teaspoon Lemon Peel Spice Rub (page 61), divided

1 cup cooked cannellini or corona beans, drained

¼ cup Liquid Gold Vegetable Stock (page 52)

10 Purple Basil Pickled Cherry Tomatoes (page 103), drained

¼ cup kalamata olives, drained

2 tablespoons capers, drained

4 teaspoons extra virgin olive oil

Makes 4 servings

Preheat the oven to 400°F.

At the food preparation station, wash the celery and cut into large chunks. Wash the carrot with a washcloth to remove any dirt from the skin and slice into large coins. Peel and slice the garlic and shallots. Wash and slice the lemon. Wash the herbs. Wash and dry off the chicken thighs and season with ¼ teaspoon of Lemon Peel Spice Rub.

Line the bottom of a 4-quart glass baking dish with the celery, carrots, garlic, and shallots. Keeping the chicken dry, place it on top of the vegetables. Build around and under the thighs with beans, Liquid Gold Vegetable Stock, Purple Basil Pickled Cherry Tomatoes, olives, capers, lemon slices, thyme and oregano sprigs, and bay leaves. Raise the chicken thighs up a bit (only the bottom third of the thighs should be in the liquid). Once everything is in the pan, give the chicken a good rub with olive oil, making sure the skin is evenly coated. Sprinkle with the remaining ¼ teaspoon of Lemon Peel Spice Rub.

Place the pan on the top rack of the oven. Bake for 50 to 60 minutes, until the skin is crisp to the touch and golden.

TIPS

If you are not a fan of chicken thighs, you can substitute bone-in and skin-on breasts, but increase the cook time as they are generally larger.

If you did not make the Purple Basil Pickled Tomatoes, you can substitute fresh cherry tomatoes.

Strawberries

One year, we were lucky enough to have a stand next to Winters Farms, a farm stand specializing in berries and corn. That summer, I learned some important strawberry secrets. If strawberries are harvested after a rain, they look beautiful but taste like water. Instead, buy or pick strawberries after a hot day with no rain. Also, wait to buy berries until the week after the season begins, because they will be more flavorful as a result of longer sun exposure. Finally, Hood berries are the hardest kind of strawberry to grow, but the results are fantastic and they are the best for jams. The berry leaves and tops contain minerals, such as iron and calcium; while these are often eaten in smoothies, this chapter highlights incorporating them into a savory salad dressing.

Canned

STRAWBERRY RHUBARB HOT SAUCE

I made this sauce as a one-time market special highlighting rhubarb, but it has now become a favorite. We make only twenty bottles once a year to celebrate the beautiful Hood strawberries that grow in June. The unique flavor combinations bring tart, sweet, spicy, and savory all together. Any variety of rhubarb can be used, but we are known for our crimson red rhubarb here in the Pacific Northwest.

1 pound fresh strawberries (about 3 cups)

3 tablespoons cane sugar

6 stalks rhubarb

½ pound red jalapeños (about 1 cup)

1 yellow onion

3 garlic cloves

1 teaspoon fenugreek seeds

1 teaspoon mustard seeds

1 teaspoon coriander seeds

2 cups rice vinegar

1½ tablespoons kosher salt

¼ teaspoon turmeric powder

¼ teaspoon cumin powder

Makes 8 half-pints

Assemble the canning stations as described on pages 5–7, steps 2–4. At the food preparation station, wash the strawberries and remove the tops. Set the tops aside for the Strawberry Top Salad Dressing recipe on page 115. In a medium bowl, macerate the strawberries and cane sugar with a potato masher. Wash and roughly chop the rhubarb; compost the leaf ends as they contain oxalic acid and are not recommended for human consumption. Wash the peppers and pop off the stems, leaving them whole. Peel and dice the onion and garlic. Grind the fenugreek seeds, mustard seeds, and coriander seeds into a fine powder with a mortar and pestle or a spice grinder.

In a large saucepan, place the vinegar, rhubarb, red jalapeños, onion, garlic, and salt. Bring to a boil over high heat, about 2 minutes. Once boiling, lower the heat to medium-high and add all the spices. Simmer uncovered for 6 minutes, until the rhubarb breaks apart with the tap of a wooden spoon.

Add the macerated strawberries to the saucepan. Blend the contents of the pan in a blender until there are no visible seeds or skins, about 4 to 6 minutes.

At the filling station, keep the jars and sauce hot while filling each jar. Use a funnel to pour the sauce directly into the jar, leaving ½ inch of headspace. Remove the air pockets, wipe the rim, and secure the lid. Place the jars in the water bath, covered by 1 inch of water. Once the water is boiling, process for 10 minutes (pages 11–14, steps 7–12).

Canned

STRAWBERRY TAMARIND CHUTNEY

Tamarind is a fruit that grows on trees and looks like a dried bean pod. It is tart in flavor and sticky in texture and is available in a paste or a concentrate that looks like molasses. The sour flavor of tamarind pairs nicely with ripe, sweet strawberries. This chutney is sugar-free, but feels like an indulgent treat due to the reduction time. It is perfect paired with a creamy Brie cheese.

2 cups strawberries

½ cup plus 1 tablespoon fresh lime juice, divided (from about 3 large limes)

2-inch piece ginger, peeled, finely minced

1 large red onions, diced (about 2 cups)

4 garlic cloves, minced

4 red chili peppers

2 tablespoons plus ½ cup white balsamic vinegar

2 tablespoons tamarind paste

1 teaspoon salt

Makes 6 quarter-pints

Assemble the canning stations as described on pages 5–7, steps 2–4. At the food preparation station, wash the strawberries and remove the tops, saving the tops for the Strawberry Top Salad Dressing recipe on page 115. Macerate the berries by mashing with a potato masher. Wash and juice the limes. Add 1 tablespoon lime juice to the berries.

(CONTINUED)

(CONTINUED)

Peel and dice the onions and peel and mince the garlic. Wash the chili peppers and remove the stems, leaving the seeds.

In a medium, heavy-bottom saucepan, place 2 tablespoons vinegar and cook over medium heat. Once hot, add the onions and ginger and sauté for 3 minutes, stirring occasionally to avoid sticking. Add the peppers and garlic and sauté another 3 minutes. Add the remaining ½ cup vinegar, the remaining ½ cup lime juice, strawberries, tamarind paste, and salt. Lower the heat and simmer for 15 minutes, stirring occasionally.

At the filling station, keep the jars and chutney hot while filling each jar. Use a funnel and spoon to fill each jar, leaving ¼ inch of headspace. Remove the air pockets, wipe the rim, and secure the lid. Place the jars in the water bath, covered by 1 inch of water. Once the water is boiling, process for 10 minutes (pages 11–14, steps 7–12).

Preserved

STRAWBERRY CUCUMBER FREEZER JAM

This is the only jam in which I use store-bought pectin, because the cold fruit pectin helps set the jam, while keeping the cooling, crisp attributes of the cucumber. When working with strawberries, I find it best to macerate them by letting them sit in the sugar and lemon for a few minutes. I made this jam for a local doughnut shop and the owners filled their churros with it for a lovely sweet and spicy treat.

1½ pounds strawberries

2¼ cups blended cucumber (about 1 pound, 5 ounces cucumbers)

¼ cup plus 1 tablespoon fresh lemon juice, divided (from about 2 small lemons)

2 cups plus 3 tablespoons cane sugar

9 tablespoons real fruit instant pectin

1 ½ teaspoons kosher salt

3 fresh red Thai chilies

Makes 6 half-pints

Wash the freezer-safe jars or plastic half-pints. At the preparation station, wash the strawberries and remove the tops, reserving the tops for the Strawberry Top Salad Dressing recipe on page 115. Peel and seed the cucumbers, reserving the peels and seeds for the Cucumber and Basil-Infused Gin recipe on page 145; then blend the cucumbers in a blender. Wash and juice the lemons.

In a large glass mixing bowl, whisk together 2 cups of cane sugar, pectin, and 1 teaspoon of salt until evenly mixed. Set aside.

In a 4-quart glass baking dish, place the strawberries, the remaining 3 tablespoons of cane sugar, and 1 tablespoon of lemon juice. Use a potato masher to combine; let sit for 10 minutes.

While the strawberries are macerating, put the blended cucumber, chilies, and the remaining ¼ cup of lemon juice into the blender and process on high until smooth. Add the strawberry and cucumber mixtures to the bowl. Mix well for 3 minutes. Use a funnel and ladle to fill each jar, leaving 1 inch of headspace, if freezing the recipe. This jam can be stored in the refrigerator for up to 3 months or frozen for up to 1 year.

TIP

Check the baking/canning aisle of your grocery store for real fruit instant pectin (see Stocking Your Pantry on page 212).

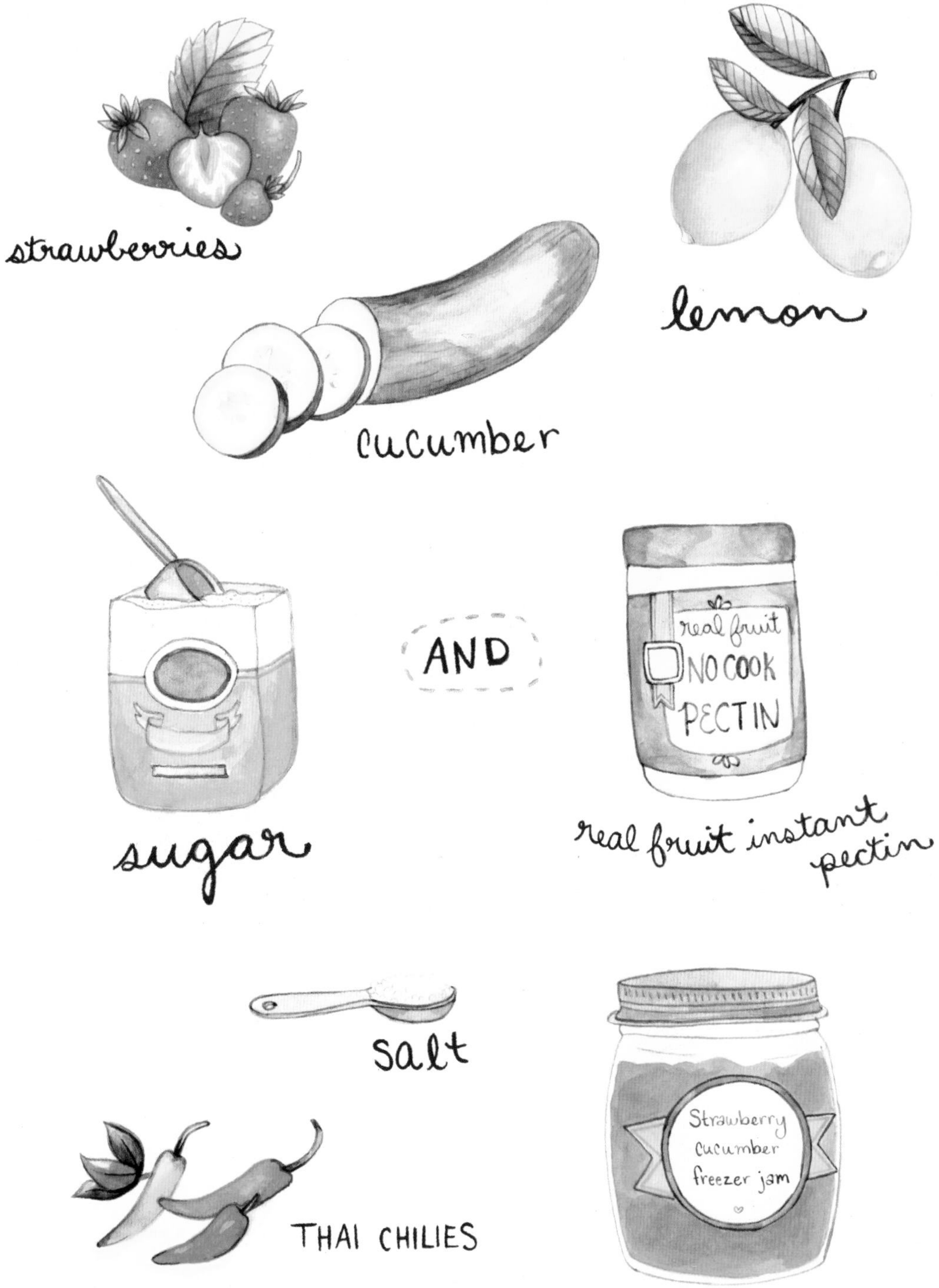

strawberries

lemon

cucumber

AND

real fruit
NO COOK
PECTIN

sugar

real fruit instant pectin

salt

THAI CHILIES

Preserved

STRAWBERRY TOP SALAD DRESSING

My grandmother once sat on a strawberry while we were berry-picking together. I was six years old and it was just about the funniest thing I had ever seen. She found it funny, too, and wiggled her bum at me, instigating the giggle fest all over again. To this day I can't go berry-picking without laughing to myself. This salad dressing is rich and creamy while at the same time tangy and sweet. It's perfect for any salad from Caesar to Cobb.

2 egg yolks

¼ cup strawberry tops (reserved from Strawberry Cucumber Freezer Jam, page 111)

¼ cup basil, chiffonade

3 tablespoons red wine vinegar

2 tablespoons dry white wine

2 tablespoons plain yogurt

2 tablespoons grated Parmigiano-Reggiano

1 teaspoon kosher salt

2 medium garlic cloves, peeled

4 Kalamata olives, pitted

⅔ cup extra virgin olive oil

Makes 1½ cups

Except for the olive oil, place all the ingredients in a food processor and pulse six times. Scrape the sides down. Turn the processor back on and slowly drizzle the olive oil through the spout and blend until emulsified. Bottle in a glass jar fitted with a lid and store in the refrigerator for up to 5 days.

TIPS

Use this salad dressing to make the Radicchio and Arugula Salad (above).

If you don't have the strawberry tops, substitute fresh basil.

Recipe

RADICCHIO AND ARUGULA SALAD

Soaking radicchio in ice water helps to eliminate the bitter taste it is known for. Give yourself plenty of time, as radicchio needs a solid two hours for soaking. I learned this technique from Cathy Whimms, the chef and owner of Nostrana in Portland. The nuttiness of the pepitas (toasted pumpkin seeds) pairs nicely with the Parmigiano cheese. Chicory flowers are bright blue flowers that grow along our wooded roadsides; they are edible and easy to gather when in bloom. If you can't find them, replace this ingredient with any edible flower.

1 medium head radicchio

2 cups arugula

¼ cup pepitas

½ cup Strawberry Top Salad Dressing (left)

¼ cup Parmigiano-Reggiano, grated

2 chicory flowers (optional)

Makes 4 servings

At the preparation station, wash the radicchio and arugula. Cut the core from the head of radicchio. Slice the head into ½-inch-thick ribbons. Fill a large bowl halfway with water and add 14 ice cubes. Place the radicchio in the bowl and let soak for 2 hours.

Drain the water out of the bowl and place the radicchio and arugula on a kitchen towel to dry. Shake off any excess water, if necessary.

In a large bowl, toss the radicchio, arugula, pepitas, and Strawberry Top Salad Dressing until well coated. Top with cheese and chicory petals.

TIP

Chicory flowers grow on the radicchio plant. They are edible and the petals bring a beautiful blue element to the salad.

Vegetables: Root to Top

Beets

We get all of our root vegetables from a farm just inside the Oregon coastline. DeNoble Family Farms is in Tillamook and grows the best root vegetables. This farm is perched on land that was once a dairy farm. The result is exceptionally fertile soil that produces huge, tasty underground vegetables, full of earthy flavor. Beets are bursting with nitrates that help to promote oxygen-rich blood, which gives you greater endurance during exercise. If you are not a beet fan, start with the golden beets, which have a much milder, earthy flavor. The beet leaves and stems—which are traditionally cast aside for the compost pile—are full of minerals and fiber. This chapter will inspire ideas of using beet stems as a vegetable dye and using the leaves for tasty dolmas.

Canned

WHOLE-GRAIN ROASTED BEET MUSTARD

The deep wine color and earthy aroma of this mustard makes my mouth water every time I pull it out of the cupboard. It is perfect for a quick snack or party hors d'oeuvres, and I love to slather it on fresh-baked bread and top it with goat cheese. Roasting the beets brings a balanced sweetness to the spicy whole-grain mustard seeds, while the balsamic vinegar gives it a wonderful depth. Your bread will forever thank you!

2 pounds beets (about 5 medium beets)

2 tablespoons extra virgin olive oil

1 tablespoon plus 1 teaspoon kosher salt, divided

8 medium garlic cloves, peeled

8 tablespoons mustard seeds

½ cup mustard powder

1 cup balsamic vinegar, divided

Makes 6 half-pints

Preheat the oven to 400°F.

Assemble the canning stations as described on pages 5–7, steps 2–4. At the food preparation station, wash the beets and cut off the stems, saving the stems for the Beet Stem Pickled Cauliflower recipe on page 120. Wearing gloves, slice the beets in half from stem to top. Line a baking sheet with parchment paper. Arrange the beets cut-side up on the paper and drizzle with the olive oil. Rub the olive oil into the skins, flip the beets, and rub the other side. Sprinkle with ½ teaspoon salt. Roast until slightly brown, about 25 minutes. Turn the beets over, sprinkle with ½ teaspoon salt, add the garlic, and roast another 25 minutes, until fork-tender.

While the beets are roasting, soak the mustard seeds in a medium bowl with 4 cups of cold water for 10 minutes. Drain the water and set the seeds to the side on a towel. In a small bowl, whisk together the mustard powder with ½ cup of water until smooth.

Once the beets are done and cool enough to handle cut into 2-inch chunks on the parchment paper. In a large, nonreactive saucepan, place the roasted beets, roasted garlic, soaked mustard seeds, ½ cup balsamic vinegar, ½ cup water, mustard powder mixture, and the remaining tablespoon of salt. Bring to a boil over high heat for about 2 minutes, stirring occasionally to avoid sticking. Turn the heat off and let sit for 5 minutes.

Place the contents into a food processor and pulse 15 times, scraping down the sides with a rubber spatula. Run on high for 4 minutes and slowly drizzle in the remaining ½ cup balsamic vinegar.

At the filling station, keep the jars and mustard hot while filling each jar. Use a funnel to spoon the sauce directly into the jar, while pressing out air pockets, leaving ½ inch of headspace. Remove any additional air pockets, wipe the rim, and secure the lid. Place the jars in the water bath, covered by 1 inch of water. Once the water is boiling, process for 10 minutes (pages 11–14, steps 7–12).

TIP

Use this recipe to make the Beet Leaf Dolmas with Seeded Rice (page 123).

Canned

GOLDEN PICKLED BEETS

A good gateway into the world of beets begins with the golden beet. These beets are less pungent and earthy than their crimson friends, and contain a slight sweetness. This simple recipe helps to make my lunch preparation quick and easy. I pop open a jar and add these golden gems to cooked couscous and top it with fresh basil and a little hot sauce. It has become my five-minute "I forgot to make lunch" lunch.

9 medium golden beets, cubed (about 8 cups)

3 cups apple cider vinegar

3 tablespoons Khmeli-Suneli Georgian Spice Blend (page 91)

3 tablespoons maple syrup

Makes 6 pints

Assemble the canning stations as described on pages 5–7, steps 2–4. At the food preparation station, wash the beets and cut off the stems and leaves, saving the stems and leaves for the Beet Leaf Dolmas with Seeded Rice recipe on page 123.

Place the beets into a medium saucepan and cover with water by 2 inches. Bring the water to a boil over high heat. Boil the beets for 30 minutes, until fork-tender. Place the beets into a bowl of cool water. Once cool to the touch, put on gloves and peel off the beet skin by running your fingers along the outside. With a paring knife, cut off any tough or grooved dark spots. Cut into 1-inch cubes.

Combine the vinegar, 1½ cups of water, and Khmeli-Suneli spice blend in a large, nonreactive saucepan and bring to a boil over high heat. Once boiling, turn the heat down and simmer and let the brine infuse for 5 minutes. Add the beets and simmer another 2 minutes. Stir in the maple syrup. Turn the heat down to the lowest setting.

At the filling station, keep the jars and beets hot while filling each jar. Pour the brine through a fine-mesh strainer into a heat-resistant pitcher, holding the beets in the pot with a slotted spoon. Spoon the spices into the bottom of the jars. With a slotted spoon and funnel, scoop the hot beets into the jar, leaving 1 inch of headspace.

Use the pitcher to fill the jar with brine, leaving ½ inch of headspace. Remove the air pockets, add more brine if necessary, wipe the rim, and secure the lid. Place the jars in the water bath, covered by 1 inch of water. Once the water is boiling, process for 10 minutes (pages 11–14, steps 7–12).

TIP

While you can find Khmeli-Suneli (page 91) in specialty stores, making your own is fun and easy.

TIP

If you do not have leftover beet stems, you can substitute with 1 tablespoon of fresh shredded beets. However, this will bring more of a beet flavor to your pickles than the beet stems do.

Canned

BEET STEM PICKLED CAULIFLOWER

Beet stems are a natural food coloring that can be used for pickling and other kitchen projects. Red beet stems will also add a wonderful orchid hue to your pickle without bringing in a beet flavor. In this recipe, the red color in the beet stems escapes into the brine and gives a pink aura to the cauliflower. This technique also works nicely with red chard stems. These bright brassicas add exotic color to any pickle plate.

2 pounds white cauliflower (from 2 medium heads)

1 cup beet stems (reserved from Whole-Grain Roasted Beet Mustard, page 119)

1 large lemon

4 cups white balsamic vinegar

2 tablespoons kosher salt

½ teaspoon whole black peppercorns

½ teaspoon coriander seeds

½ teaspoon yellow mustard seeds

½ teaspoon crushed red pepper flakes

¼ teaspoon fennel seeds

¼ teaspoon cumin seeds

Makes 6 pints

Assemble the canning stations as described on pages 5–7, steps 2–4. At the food preparation station, wash the cauliflower, beet stems, and lemon under cold running water. Cut out the stems and leaves from the cauliflower and dice the stems

(CONTINUED)

(CONTINUED)
and leaves into ¼-inch pieces. Using the tip of a paring knife, break down the florets into 1-inch pieces. Dice the beet stems into ¼-inch pieces. Slice the lemon into ¼-inch-thick rounds.

Place the white balsamic vinegar, 3 cups of water, salt, and spices in a large, nonreactive saucepan and bring the brine to a boil over high heat. Once it begins to boil, turn the heat down to low and steep for 10 minutes. Add the cauliflower pieces and beet stems to the brine. Return to a boil over high heat, then turn the heat down to the lowest setting and let it sit for 5 minutes.

At the filling station, keep the jars and brine hot while filling each jar. Pour the brine through a fine-mesh strainer into a heat-resistant pitcher. Then spoon the spices from the strainer into the bottom of the jars before adding the cauliflower and topping with brine. With a slotted spoon and a funnel, scoop the hot cauliflower and beet stems into the jar. When the jars are about halfway full, add a slice of lemon against the side of each jar, ensuring visibility. Continue to fill each jar with cauliflower, leaving 1 inch of headspace. Use the pitcher to fill the jar with brine, leaving ½ inch of headspace. Remove the air pockets, add more brine if necessary, wipe the rim, and secure the lid. Place the jars in the water bath, covered by 1 inch of water. Once the water is boiling, process for 10 minutes (pages 11–14, steps 7–12).

TIP →
If you did not make the Whole-Grain Roasted Beet Mustard, substitute with your favorite whole-grain mustard.

Recipe

BEET LEAF DOLMAS WITH SEEDED RICE

On Mondays at our commercial kitchen, we gather for "veggie lunch." Three small businesses come together to feast, chat, and check in. My husband makes these dolmas for the lunch on a regular basis and they are always a hit. I prefer beet leaves for this recipe to the traditional grape leaves because they are more tender and I love their beautiful color. The key to making these dolmas is rolling the rice tightly in the plastic wrap, which helps to create a compact, tiny package.

1 cup jasmine rice

2 tablespoons Whole-Grain Roasted Beet Mustard (page 119)

1 teaspoon radish sprout seeds

½ teaspoon yellow mustard seeds

½ teaspoon kosher salt, divided

¼ cup plus 1 tablespoon fresh lemon juice, divided

3 tablespoons white balsamic vinegar, divided

¼ cup plus 1 tablespoon olive oil, divided

20 large beet leaves

Makes 20 dolmas

In a medium saucepan fitted with a lid, combine the rice, the Whole-Grain Roasted Beet Mustard, radish sprout seeds, mustard seeds, ¼ teaspoon salt, and 1¾ cups of water; stir the ingredients together, then bring the contents to a boil over high heat. Once boiling, turn the heat to low and cover. Cook for 20 minutes. Remove the lid and fluff with a fork, mixing the seeds evenly through the rice.

In a small bowl, mix 1 tablespoon lemon juice, 1 tablespoon vinegar, and 1 tablespoon olive oil. Pour over the rice and let it cool.

At the food preparation station, wash the beet leaves under cold running water and discard any leaves that are discolored. Make an ice-water bath by placing 4 cups of cold water and 4 ice cubes in a medium bowl and set aside.

Bring 4 cups of water to a boil in a medium skillet over high heat; add the leaves to the boiling water, without overlapping them, and blanch for 1 minute. Remove the leaves with a slotted spoon and place them in the ice-water bath to stop the cooking process.

Take 1 leaf (if leaves are on the small side, overlap 2 leaves) out of the ice-water bath and dry between 2 towels. Set the leaf aside on a dry cutting board. Lay down a piece of plastic wrap, place 1 tablespoon of rice in the center, fold the plastic wrap over the rice, and press with fingers and thumbs to form a small brick of rice. Peel off the wrap and place the rice in the lower center of the leaf. Fold the small end up and tuck in the empty sides of the leaf toward the center. Keep folding until it can be rolled. Place the dolma into a 2-quart glass baking dish. Continue rolling and stacking until done.

Whisk together the remaining ¼ cup lemon juice, ¼ cup olive oil, 2 tablespoons vinegar, and ¼ teaspoon salt. Pour over the dolmas. Refrigerate for at least 2 hours, or overnight.

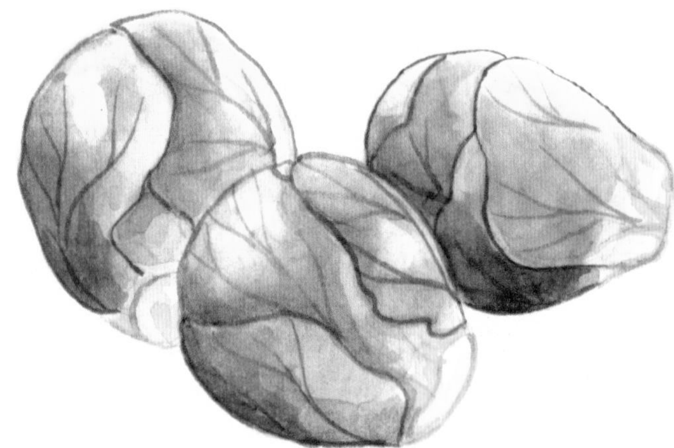

Brussels Sprouts

These fiber-packed brassicas are officially the most hated vegetable on the Internet. However, I will take a stand for these delicious tiny cabbages. Brussels sprouts get a bad name because they are often boiled and overcooked, resulting in a sulfur-smelling, tasteless version of themselves. Shaved Brussels are my favorite and I encourage you to give them a try. These leafy greens are rich in nutrients and vitamins, and appear at the market from fall through winter. Often mispronounced as "Brussel sprouts," they indeed originate from the city of Brussels and are pronounced so.

Canned

PICKLED BRUSSELS AND ROMANESCO GIARDINIERA

I get a kick out of pickling vegetables that people find mysterious. Romanesco keeps my pickling game interesting and educational because it creates an opportunity to teach people about the vegetable throughout the year. This strange-looking relative of cauliflower gives this condiment a twist on a classic giardiniera, an Italian relish of pickled vegetables. It is the perfect addition to anything from hoagies to pizza.

2 pounds Brussels sprouts

2 heads romanesco

4 tablespoons kosher salt

4 cups red wine vinegar

1 tablespoon yellow mustard seeds

1 tablespoon dried mint

1 tablespoon dried oregano

¼ teaspoon ground black pepper

1 tablespoon crushed red pepper flakes

1 teaspoon cayenne pepper

Makes 6 pints

Assemble the canning stations as described on pages 5–7, steps 2–4. At the food preparation station, wash the Brussels sprouts and romanesco under cold running water (check for bugs; they like to hide in there!). Cut out the stem and leaves from the romanesco and set aside for the Romanesco Leaf Sauerkraut recipe on page 129.

Using the tip of the knife, break down the florets into 1-inch pieces. Trim the end off the Brussels and compost any discolored or wilted leaves. Cut in half lengthwise. Place flat-side down and cut into ribbons, starting at the base and moving to the top.

Place the Brussels and the romanesco in a large bowl. Add the salt and 4 tablespoons of cold tap water. Gently massage the vegetables for 3 minutes. Place in the refrigerator for 15 minutes.

While the vegetables sit, combine the red wine vinegar, 3 cups of water, mustard seeds, mint, oregano, and black pepper in a large, nonreactive saucepan. Bring the brine to a boil over high heat. Once hot and bubbling, turn the heat down to low and let steep for 10 minutes.

Drain the water from the bowl by placing a plate over the top and tipping the bowl to the side (this keeps the salt on the vegetables to ensure a crispier pickle). Wearing gloves, massage the red pepper flakes and cayenne into the Brussels and romanesco.

At the filling station, keep the jars and brine hot while filling each jar. Pour the brine through a fine-mesh sieve into a heat-resistant pitcher. Put a spoonful of spices from the strainer into the bottom of the jar. Using your hands and a funnel, pack the vegetables into the jar, pressing down in order to pack it full. Top the jar with brine, leaving ½ inch of headspace. Remove the air pockets by holding the vegetables down with the back of a spoon and gently tapping the jar on a kitchen towel. Add brine if necessary, wipe the rim, and secure the lid. Place the jars in the water bath, covered by 1 inch of water. Once the water is boiling, process for 10 minutes (pages 11–14, steps 7–12).

Canned

WHITE WINE–PICKLED BRUSSELS SPROUTS

These brassicas pop up at our farmers' markets in September, and I love seeing shoppers with long stalks of Brussels sticking out of their market bags. Most Brussels are destined for roasting, but in this recipe they are roasted and then pickled. Roasting before pickling adds a slightly caramelized flavor and keeps the sprouts from taking on a soggy, boiled texture. The earthy flavor of the Brussels pairs well with the small red pequin chilies, which lend a slightly smoky finish to these pickled Brussels.

3 pounds Brussels sprouts

1 tablespoon olive oil

¼ teaspoon plus 2 tablespoons kosher salt, divided

1 cup distilled vinegar

2½ cups rice vinegar

2 cups dry white wine

2 tablespoons Orange Peel Pickling Spice (page 75)

6 dried pequin chilies

Makes 6 pints

Prepare the canning stations as described on pages 5–7, steps 2–4. At the preparation station, wash the Brussels sprouts under cold running water. Remove and compost any brown spots and wilted leaves. Slice the Brussels in half from stem to top.

Preheat the oven to 350°F.

On a lined baking sheet, lay the Brussels flat-side up and drizzle with olive oil and ¼ teaspoon salt; rub in the oil with your fingers. Roast for 20 minutes. Using tongs, flip and roast for another 30 minutes.

In a medium saucepan, place the distilled vinegar, rice vinegar, white wine, 1 cup of water, Orange Peel Pickling Spice, and the remaining 2 tablespoons salt. Bring to a boil over high heat. Once boiling, turn the heat to low and let steep for 10 minutes.

At the filling station, keep the jars and brine hot while filling each jar. Pour the brine through a fine-mesh strainer into a heat-resistant pitcher. Spoon the spices from the strainer into each jar, add 1 pequin chili, and pack the Brussels in tightly, leaving 1 inch of headspace. Use a funnel to fill the jar with brine, leaving ½ inch of headspace. Remove the air pockets, add brine if necessary, press Brussels down with the back of a spoon, wipe the rim, and secure the lid. Place the jars in the water bath, covered by 1 inch of water. Once the water is boiling, process for 10 minutes (pages 11–14, steps 7–12).

TIPS

If you did not make the Orange Peel Pickling Spice, substitute with another pickling spice.

Use this recipe to make the Haluski with Blackened Brussels (page 130).

ATLAS
PEPPER MILL IMPORTS
MADE IN GREECE

Preserved

ROMANESCO LEAF SAUERKRAUT

I use this technique for just about any cabbage and green food scraps I have in the kitchen. While you can make this sauerkraut with a jar and a baggie full of water, there are also helpful supplies listed in Stocking Your Pantry (page 212). This recipe involves weighing your green ingredients to ensure accuracy. You can substitute other spices, in place of the caraway and cayenne, or keep it classic.

4 cups (400 grams) trimmed leaves and stalks from greens reserved from Lemon Spring Green Sauce, page 159)

1 cup (300 grams) shredded cabbage

2 medium garlic cloves

1 tablespoon kosher salt

1 teaspoon caraway seeds

½ teaspoon cayenne pepper

Makes 1 quart jar

Wash the romanesco leaves and stalks under cold running water. Remove the remaining dirt with a washcloth. Slice the leaves into ¼-inch-thin ribbons. Finely dice the stalks. Wash and shred the cabbage. Peel and thinly slice the garlic. Place the leaves, stalks, cabbage, and garlic in a large bowl. Wearing gloves, massage in the salt, caraway, and cayenne for 5 minutes. Let the bowl sit for 20 minutes.

Spoon the vegetables into a 32-ounce jar, packing them down by hand. Pour in any remaining liquid from the bowl. Clean 1 inch of headspace with a kitchen towel, ensuring that no particles are sticking out of the brine.

Place a fermenting weight into the jar to keep the vegetables submerged. Put 2 tablespoons of water into the plastic fermenting top and place it on the jar. Place the jar into a shallow bowl to catch any overflow liquid that might be produced.

Let it sit on the counter for 24 hours. After 24 hours, if the vegetables are not covered by water, create a salt solution with ½ teaspoon of kosher salt and 1 cup of water. Top off the jar. Let it ferment another 24 hours. Store the jar in the refrigerator for up to 14 days.

TIPS

If you don't have a fermenting weight, use a baggie with ½ cup of water, tied tightly.

Use a wide-mouth quart jar for easier packing.

Recipe

HALUSKI WITH BLACKENED BRUSSELS

Sometimes I find a favorite recipe while looking through new cookbooks, and sometimes I discover a beloved family recipe that could have easily slipped away. This haluski recipe was passed on to my cousin Abraham by our grandmother, and when he came to visit me in Portland he taught me how to make it. Haluski is a Polish dish classically made with cabbage, butter, and noodles. In this remake, I liven it up with blackened, pickled Brussels and locally produced kielbasa.

1 small head green cabbage

1 pound kielbasa sausage ring

1 large garlic clove

1 half-pint jar White Wine Pickled Brussels Sprouts (page 127)

2 teaspoons kosher salt, divided

8 ounces egg noodles

¼ cup plus 1 tablespoon salted butter, divided

1 teaspoon sweet paprika

1 teaspoon cayenne pepper

¼ teaspoon fresh ground black pepper

2 tablespoons chopped fresh flat parsley

Makes 4 servings

At the preparation station, remove any bruised or discolored outer layers from the head of the cabbage and compost or store in the freezer for making stock. Wash the cabbage under cold running water. Cut the cabbage in half from top to bottom, cutting through the core. Cut out the core and set it aside. Slice the remaining cabbage halves into thin slices about ½ inch thick.

Remove the casing from the sausage and slice the sausage into ½-inch rounds. Peel the garlic and mince. Open the jar of White Wine Pickled Brussels Sprouts and drain off the pickling liquid. Set the Brussels sprouts on a kitchen towel and pat dry. This will help to give them a nice char.

In a medium saucepan, boil 6 cups of water and 1 teaspoon of kosher salt. Boil the noodles as directed on the package, about 8 minutes.

While the water is boiling, melt ¼ cup butter in a large skillet over medium heat. Once melted, add the cabbage, garlic, and the remaining 1 teaspoon salt. Cook for 5 minutes, stirring occasionally. Add the spices and sauté for 5 minutes.

As the cabbage is cooking, melt 1 tablespoon butter in a small skillet over medium-high heat. Place the Brussels and sausage, cut-side down, in the butter. Let sit untouched for 4 minutes, flip over once they're brown and crisp, and let them cook for 2 minutes. Remove from the pan and let them rest on a kitchen towel.

Drain the noodles and place in the skillet. Add the sausage and heat until everything is well combined, about 2 minutes. Plate and top with the blackened Brussels and garnish with parsley.

TIP

If you did not make the White Wine Pickled Brussels Sprouts, replace with fresh Brussels, steamed until soft. Dry and blacken as directed.

Carrots

Carrots create a wonderful canning opportunity because they have two growing seasons. If you forget to pickle them in the summer, you will have a chance again in the fall. They grow and are harvested easily, making carrots a perfect fresh vegetable for local community food programs. My mother started the Providence Employee Garden, which donates 2,600 pounds of produce a year, especially carrots, lettuce, and fruit. Fresh food is harvested directly by the volunteers who grow it and it's given to community members who need it. Rich in protein and vitamins, the carrot tops and peels are often discarded but, if properly cleaned, they can be added to many meals, packing your table full of potassium and calcium.

Carrot Cumin
Slaw, page 135.

TIP
Use these pickles to make the Pork Banh Mi recipe (page 139).

Canned

HABAÑERO PICKLED CARROTS, DAIKON, AND LOTUS ROOT

When I first started pickling in our tiny 700-square-foot house, my husband hated it. He hated pickles, he hated vinegar, and he would hold his shirt over his nose while I frantically stuffed things into jars. Little did we both know that ten years down the road it would become our business and our shared passion. Now, he loves the pickling process and has seen me pickle just about everything. Some experiments have achieved great results while others were disasters Turns out, not everything makes a good pickle. The ugly: pickled green strawberries. The bad: pickled seaweed. The good: pickled lotus root.

1 pound daikon

1 pound lotus root

3 pounds carrots

9 cups seasoned rice vinegar

8 tablespoons salt

7 cinnamon sticks, divided

7 whole star anise pods, divided

3 fresh habañeros, cut in half

Makes 6 pints

Assemble the canning stations as described on pages 5–7, steps 2–4. At the food preparation station, wash the vegetables under cold running water. Peel the daikon and slice into ¼-inch-thick matchsticks (length needs to be 2 inches shorter than the top of the jar). Peel the lotus root with a knife and slice thinly into ¼-inch-thick coins. Cut the carrots into ¼-inch-thick matchsticks (the same length as the daikon). Place the vegetables into separate bowls and cover with cold water.

In a large stainless steel saucepan, place the vinegar, 4 cups of water, salt, 1 cinnamon stick, and 1 star anise pod. Bring to a boil over high heat, until the salt dissolves, about 3 minutes. Turn the heat down to low and let the brine simmer for 10 minutes.

At the filling station, remove the hot jars from the canning pot and, in each one, place 1 cinnamon stick, 1 star anise, and half a habañero into the bottom of a jar. Pack the vegetables into the jars, leaving 1 inch of headspace from the top. Pour the brine into a heat-resistant pitcher and use a funnel to cover the vegetables with brine, leaving ¼ inch of headspace. Place the jars in the water bath, covered by 1 inch of water. Once the water is boiling, process for 10 minutes (pages 11–14, steps 7–12).

TIPS

You can use multicolored carrots for this recipe to create a visually stunning effect. If you use purple carrots, the brine turns a vivid magenta. The carrots themselves lose the purple color over time, but they will still taste delicious.

When canning, sugar helps to keep the color in your fruits and vegetables. It also takes the edge off the vinegar. I leave it out of most pickling recipes because I love the vinegar bite, but if you like a balanced pickle, add 2 tablespoons of cane sugar to your brine with the salt.

Canned

CARROT CUMIN SLAW

Whether adding it to quinoa bowls, placing it in sandwiches, or tucking it into pita pockets, this slaw has become a lunchtime essential. White wine contributes a balancing acidity but in a gentle way that keeps it from veering into the realm of a pickle. Cumin and dill seeds inject a herbaceous complexity, while the peppers and carrots hold a lovely sweetness. This slaw is both earthy and crunchy. Say hello to your new favorite pantry staple. (See photo on page 133.)

4 pounds carrots (about 6 cups julienned)

2 orange bell peppers

2 red fresno peppers

1 tablespoon cumin seeds

1 teaspoon dill seeds

3 cups plus 2 tablespoons white wine vinegar, divided

6 garlic cloves

2 tablespoons kosher salt

1 tablespoon sweet paprika

1 tablespoon crushed red pepper flakes

1 teaspoon ground cinnamon

3 cups dry white wine

Makes 6 pints

Assemble the canning stations as described on pages 5–7, steps 2–4. At the food preparation station, wash the carrots and peppers under cold running water. Cut the carrots into 3-inch-long matchsticks (see the Chopping Chart on page 9).
(CONTINUED)

(CONTINUED)

Cut the bell peppers into equal width, about 3-inch-long pieces. Slice the red fresno peppers into ¼-inch whole slices. Peel and thinly slice the garlic.

In a large, nonreactive saucepan over medium-high heat, toast the cumin and dill seeds until fragrant, and place on a plate. Using the same saucepan, add 2 tablespoons vinegar. On medium-high heat, sauté the carrots, peppers, garlic, and the remaining spices (including toasted cumin and dill) for 10 minutes, until the carrots begin to soften. Add the white wine and the remaining 3 cups vinegar, and bring to a boil over high heat. Once boiling, reduce the heat to the lowest setting.

At the filling station, keep the jars and carrots hot while filling each jar. Using a slotted spoon and funnel, place the pieces into the jar and pack down with a spoon, leaving 1 inch of headspace. Use a heat-resistant pitcher to fill the jars with brine to cover the carrots, leaving ½ inch of headspace. Remove the air pockets by gently tapping the jars on a kitchen towel. Add brine if necessary, wipe the rim, and secure the lid. Place the jars in the water bath, covered by 1 inch of water. Once the water is boiling, process for 10 minutes (pages 11–14, steps 7–12).

Preserved

CARROT TOP HAZELNUT PESTO

The Pacific Northwest is in love with hazelnuts. We have hazelnut beer, hazelnut candy, and our pigs are even raised on a strict diet of hazelnuts. One year our farmers' market booth was next to Freddy Guy's Hazelnuts, and we spent the summer savoring their beautifully roasted hazelnuts. This hazelnut pesto recipe is my all-time favorite. We toss it with vegetables and pasta and let the vegetables warm the olive oil and bring this delicious pesto to life.

Tops from one bunch carrots, about 4 ounces (reserved from Carrot Cumin Slaw, page 135)

4 ounces fresh basil

1 ounce flat-leaf parsley

6 medium garlic cloves

½ cup roasted hazelnuts, skin on

½ cup fresh lemon juice (from 4 large lemons)

1 tablespoon kosher salt

1½ cups extra virgin olive oil

Makes 5 quarter-pints

At the food preparation station, fill a large bowl halfway with cold water. Place the carrot tops in the bowl and submerge underwater. Rinse gently to remove any dirt. Wash the basil and parsley under cold running water and remove any brown stems. Peel the garlic.

Place all the greens in a food processor and pulse 6 times. Open the lid and scrape down the mixture with a rubber spatula. Add the garlic, hazelnuts, lemon juice, and salt. Secure the lid and pulse 6 more times. Open and scrape down the sides. Add ½ cup olive oil, secure the lid again, and turn on the processor. While running, slowly drizzle in the remaining olive oil.

Place the pesto into clean glass jars and store in the refrigerator for up to 1 week or in the freezer for up to 6 months.

TIPS

If you made the Habañero Pickled Carrots, Daikon, and Lotus Root recipe and want to use all the carrot tops, this recipe will need to be tripled; do it in three separate batches, so the food processor does not overflow.

Use this recipe to make the Pork Banh Mi (page 139).

You can substitute any nut for the hazelnuts—I often use sunflower seeds.

Recipe

PORK BANH MI

We moved to a new house eight years ago. Our old neighborhood had the typical chain grocery stores, while our new one had Overseas Taste, Portland Mercado, and Fubon. The availability of these Russian, Mexican, and Asian grocery stores did amazing things for our pantry and our meals. Traditional banh mi sandwiches bring together meat, pickles, fresh vegetables, mayonnaise, and baguettes. This sandwich has these Vietnamese staples but with the addition of spices from around the world, and it perfectly reflects the various cultures of my neighborhood.

2 tablespoons smoked Spanish paprika

1 tablespoon kosher salt

1 tablespoon dried oregano (preferably Mexican), crumbled

1 teaspoon ground cumin

1 pound pork loin

2 cups fresh diced tomatoes

½ cup fresh orange juice

4 medium garlic cloves, peeled and crushed

2 cinnamon sticks

1-inch piece ginger, peeled and grated

2 tablespoons Carrot Top Hazelnut Pesto (page 136)

2 tablespoons plain yogurt

1 teaspoon apple cider vinegar

4 small Vietnamese banh mi baguettes (or 1 large French baguette, cut crosswise into four sections)

1 jar Habañero Pickled Carrots, Daikon, and Lotus Root (page 135)

1 bunch cilantro

Makes 4 servings

Preheat the oven to 350°F.

Combine the paprika, salt, oregano, and cumin in a small bowl. Rub the pork with the spice mixture until completely coated. Place the tomatoes in a Dutch oven or a roasting pan with a lid. Pour in the orange juice and place the pork loin in the center of the pan. Surround with garlic, cinnamon sticks, and ginger. Cover and roast until the meat pulls apart easily, about 3 hours. Remove and discard the cinnamon sticks. Using 2 forks, shred the pork in the Dutch oven.

Place the pesto and yogurt in a small bowl and whisk to blend. Slowly whisk in the apple cider vinegar.

Split the individual baguettes in half lengthwise, leaving one side intact. Spread the pesto mixture on all eight halves. Mound the pork on the four bottom halves. Top with pickled vegetables and garnish with cilantro leaves. Serve immediately.

TIPS

A slow cooker can also be used to make this pulled pork.

If you did not make the pickled vegetables and pesto, you can substitute with any similar pesto and pickles.

Cucumber

The Culinary Breeding Network fights food waste from the start—with the seeds. The network's approach is to grow better-tasting produce so that more will be bought, cooked, and eaten, due to its excellent quality, integrity, and flavor. At the annual variety showcase, chefs, growers, canners, and buyers all participate in the conversation. Last year, cucumbers were on the tasting panel—highlighting their star role in canning. We tasted many varieties and learned how well they hydrate the body, which in turn reduces stress. While cucumbers are most often pickled, this chapter will push them into a new role as the base for a hot sauce, inspired by my discussions at the Culinary Breeding Network.

Canned

CUCUMBER MUSTARD HOT SAUCE

TIP
Use this recipe for the Green Tomato Bloody Mary Mix (page 44).

I had no idea there were so many devoted hot sauce fans out there until we started receiving emails, gifts, and even Christmas cards. I never know when I'm going to bump into a hot sauce fanatic. I met Greg, one such spicy devotee, while at a sauce demo in an interiors store. Greg was waiting for his wife and came to my table. He tried all the sauces and wanted to take them back with him to Barbados, where he lives part-time. The next time Greg was in town, he gifted me his favorite selection of sauces from Barbados. This recipe is inspired by one of these sauces and is my tribute to Greg.

2 medium cucumbers

1 medium yellow onion

3 medium garlic cloves

3 green jalapeño peppers

6 green serrano peppers

1½ cups apple cider vinegar

1 tablespoon plus 1 teaspoon kosher salt, divided

⅔ cup Turmeric Mustard (page 188)

½ teaspoon celery salt

¼ teaspoon turmeric powder

Makes 6 half-pints

Assemble the canning stations as described on pages 5–7, steps 2–4. At the food preparation station, wash the cucumbers and peel the skins. Set the skins aside for the Mustard Lime Sandwich Slicers, opposite. Cut the cucumbers into ½-inch cubes. Peel and dice the onion and garlic. Wash the peppers under cold running water and slice into ¼-inch rounds, leaving the seeds. Set aside.

In a large saucepan, place the apple cider vinegar, 1 cup of water, and 1 tablespoon salt. Bring to a boil over high heat, about 2 minutes. Once at a boil, turn the heat down to medium-high and add the cucumbers. Simmer uncovered for 10 minutes.

In a separate pan, add ¼ cup of brine from the simmering pot and sauté the onion, garlic, and peppers. Once the onions are soft, about 10 minutes, add to the brined cucumbers in the large pot. Add the Turmeric Mustard, the remaining 1 teaspoon salt, celery salt, and turmeric powder. Simmer for 10 minutes, stirring occasionally. Turn the heat down to the lowest setting and blend the mixture in the pot with an immersion blender.

At the filling station, keep the jars and sauce hot while filling each jar. Transfer the sauce in a heat-resistant pitcher. Use a funnel and fill each jar, leaving ½ inch of headspace. Once the water is boiling, process for 10 minutes (pages 11–14, steps 7–12).

TIPS
To make homemade celery salt, grind equal parts celery seeds and kosher salt with a mortar and pestle.

If you did not make the Turmeric Mustard. you can substitute with store-bought yellow mustard.

Canned

MUSTARD LIME SANDWICH SLICERS

This recipe is like adding mustard and pickles to your sandwich all at once and is perfect for adding a pickle punch to your next sack lunch. I created these pickled slicers especially for topping a Cubano sandwich. The slicers are tart from the lime juice, tangy from the mustard, and have a deep turmeric glow. This is a good recipe to break out the mandolin for, but if you don't have one, get ready to practice your slicing skills.

6 medium cucumbers

6 medium garlic cloves

½ cup fresh lime juice (from about 4 large limes)

4 cups distilled vinegar

3 tablespoons kosher salt

1 teaspoon whole peppercorns

1 cup Turmeric Mustard (page 188)

1 tablespoon mustard seeds

¼ teaspoon turmeric powder

1½ teaspoons crushed red pepper flakes, divided

Makes 6 pints

TIP
If you didn't make the Turmeric Mustard, you can substitute with store-bought yellow mustard.

Assemble the canning stations as described on pages 5–7, steps 2–4. At the food preparation station, wash the cucumbers under cold running water. Cut the cucumbers into ¼-inch-thick slices lengthwise, then cut them to fit the length of the jar, minus an inch. Peel the garlic. Wash the limes and squeeze the juice.

In a medium, nonreactive saucepan, make the brine by combining vinegar, 2 cups of water, salt, peppercorns, lime juice, Turmeric Mustard, mustard seeds, and turmeric powder. Bring to a boil over high heat, until the salt dissolves. Turn the heat down to low and let the brine infuse for 5 minutes.

At the filling station, keep the jars and brine hot while filling each jar. Place one garlic clove and ¼ teaspoon of crushed red pepper flakes into the bottom of each jar. Tightly pack the jar with cucumber slices, leaving 1 inch of headspace from the top. Use a heat-resistant pitcher and funnel to pour the brine into the jars, leaving ½ inch of headspace. Remove the air pockets, add more brine if necessary, wipe the rim, and secure the lid. Place the jars in the water bath, covered by 1 inch of water. Once the water is boiling, process for 10 minutes (pages 11–14, steps 7–12).

TIPS

Keep the pickles crisp by adding fresh grape leaves. I weigh the pickles down by putting a blanched grape leaf into the top of each jar.

Use these pickles to make the Dan Dan Noodles (page 146).

TIP
Bottle this in quarter-pints if you're giving them out as party favors and affix a homemade Summer Gin and Tonic recipe card to each jar.

Preserved

CUCUMBER AND BASIL–INFUSED GIN

This infusion is a perfect way to use leftover cucumber peels and it absolutely screams summer! Fresh basil gives it a delicate, fresh, herbaceous lift and a lovely subtle green glow. I like to make these as cookout party favors with the Summer Gin and Tonic recipe card below. If you prefer, you can also use a potato-based vodka in place of the gin. Some liquor infusions need lots of time, but this one infuses quickly, so keep an eye on it and use it right away.

4 fresh basil leaves, lightly packed

1 cup cucumber peels and scraps (reserved from Turmeric Mustard, page 188)

3 cups gin

Makes 6 quarter-pints

At the food preparation station, wash the basil. Pat the leaves dry with a kitchen towel.

Place the cucumber peels and scraps into a quart jar. Add the basil and fill the jar with gin. Screw on the lid and place in the refrigerator.

After 24 hours, strain the liquid through a fine-mesh strainer, pressing out any excess liquid. Strain the resulting liquid through a coffee filter or a jelly bag to remove any extra bits of cucumber. Pour into clean glass jars and store in the refrigerator for up to 1 month.

TIPS

See Stocking Your Pantry (page 212) for recommended gin.

If you don't have cucumber peels from another recipe, you can substitute with 1 cup of sliced cucumber.

Recipe

Makes 1 drink

title: SUMMER GIN AND TONIC

directions:

½ cup tonic water, ¼ cup Cucumber and Basil–Infused Gin, 2 drops bitters, 1 slice lime, for garnish

Stir all the ingredients in a glass with ice. Garnish with a slice of lime and serve.

Recipe

DAN DAN NOODLES

Dan Dan noodles are a Chinese dish made with preserved vegetables and Sichuan peppercorns. These special peppercorns add to your overall experience of the dish by numbing your mouth slightly. I love their distinctive heat sensation and I have been known to pop a few in my mouth as I am cooking. This version is a fun play on tradition, using the homemade Mustard Lime Sandwich Slicers and the pickling brine instead of the traditional preserved vegetables. Enjoy these comforting noodles on particularly cold days.

1 tablespoon coconut oil

1 pound ground pork

1 teaspoon Sichuan peppercorns

¼ cup chopped water chestnuts

½ pound sliced cremini mushrooms

1½ cups Liquid Gold Vegetable Stock (page 52)

¼ cup light miso

¼ cup soy sauce

1 medium garlic clove, minced

½-inch piece ginger, peeled, finely grated

2 tablespoons pickling brine from the Mustard Lime Sandwich Slicers

10-ounce package udon noodles

1 teaspoon sesame oil

¼ cup diced Mustard Lime Sandwich Slicers (page 143)

¼ cup diced scallions

Makes 4 servings

In a large skillet over medium heat, heat the coconut oil. Once hot, add the ground pork and cook until there is no visible pink, about 5 minutes. Stir in the peppercorns, water chestnuts, and mushrooms, and let cook for 4 minutes.

In a medium bowl, mix the vegetable stock, miso, soy sauce, garlic, ginger, and pickling brine. Stir into the skillet and cook about 6 minutes to thicken.

In a large saucepan, bring salted water to a boil over high heat. Add the noodles and cook as directed on the package. Drain the noodles and rinse with cold water.

Add sesame oil to the skillet and turn off the heat. Portion the noodles into four individual serving bowls. Spoon the sauce over the noodles and top with the Mustard Lime Sandwich Slicers and scallions.

TIPS

If you did not make the pickled slicers, you can use any store-bought dill pickles and their brine.

If you did not make the Liquid Gold Vegetable Stock, substitute with any vegetable stock you have on hand.

Fennel

This aromatic plant originates in the Mediterranean and thrives in our wet Oregon climate. It can be found flowering along our Oregon highways and byways. Raw fennel has a strong, often overpowering, licorice flavor. When roasted, it gets sweet, with a subtle note of anise. While it has a tendency to take over a garden if it's not picked before it reseeds, those seeds can be picked and dried. The whole plant can be used for culinary purposes from the bulb, stalk, and fronds to the flowering seeds. The often-wasted fronds are full of fiber that can help lower cholesterol.

TIP
Use wide-mouth pint jars to fit the width of the fennel bulb and press it against the glass.

Canned

PICKLED ROASTED FENNEL BULB

Roasting vegetables before pickling them brings out their natural sweetness, concentrates all their flavors beautifully, and leaves you with a firmer vegetable. When roasting for pickling, these vegetables are done when they are golden brown; any darker than that and they will darken the brine. Every time I add this fennel bulb to a pickle plate or cheese board, it is the most talked-about vegetable. The end result of this pickle is stunning.

2 large lemons

6 medium fennel bulbs

1 teaspoon extra virgin olive oil

2 teaspoons curry powder

1 teaspoon plus 3 tablespoons kosher salt, divided

6 cups white balsamic vinegar

Makes 3 pints

Assemble the canning stations as described on pages 5–7, steps 2–4. At the food preparation station, wash the lemons and fennel under cold running water. Slice the lemons into ¼-inch-thick rounds. Trim off the fennel stalks and save them for the Roasted Fennel Stalk Curry recipe on page 152. Save the fronds for the Fennel Frond Chimichurri recipe on page 153. Slice the fennel into ¼-inch-thick slices, from top to bottom (see diagram at right).

Preheat the oven to 350°F.

Line a baking sheet with parchment paper. Lay the fennel and lemon slices onto the paper. Using a pastry brush, lightly brush the fennel and lemon with olive oil. Sprinkle with curry powder and 1 teaspoon of salt. Place the baking sheet into the oven and roast the fennel and lemon for 20 minutes.

While the vegetables are roasting, place the vinegar, 4 cups of water, and the remaining 3 tablespoons salt into a medium, nonreactive saucepan and bring to a boil over high heat. Once boiling, turn the heat down to low.

After 20 minutes of roasting, remove the baking sheet and turn over the fennel and lemons. Return to the oven and roast for 12 minutes. When each side shows some golden color, the roasting is done. If the fennel pieces are taller than 1 inch from the top of the jar, trim them with kitchen shears.

At the filling station, keep the jars and brine hot while filling each jar. Use a heat-resistant pitcher to pour ¼ inch of brine into the bottom of the jar, and stack slices of fennel and lemon against the glass. Pack the jars tight. Top with brine, leaving ¼ inch of headspace. Remove any additional air pockets, wipe the rim, and secure the lid. Place the jars in the water bath, covered by 1 inch of water. Once the water is boiling, process for 10 minutes (pages 11–14, steps 7–12).

TIPS

If you would like 6 jars, use wide-mouth half-pints and lay the slices flat.

Use this recipe to make the Scallops with Chimichurri (page 155).

Keep the base in tact and slice fennel vertically into 1/4 inch slices.

Canned

ROASTED FENNEL STALK CURRY

My friend Kusuma Rao is a personal chef and I'm continuously learning from her about the importance of layering flavors. A few years ago we hosted a class together where she gave a lesson on creating a curry and I instructed students on how to can their finished product. We were co-teachers, but I was lucky enough to also be her student. Just one day in class with her has influenced how I think about cooking and eating. I am grateful for her knowledge, friendship, and ability to create some of the best food I have ever tasted. This curry recipe is a result of watching her work to build a sauce with depth and dimension.

TIP
Use kitchen shears to dice your fennel stalks into ¼-inch pieces. If they are any larger than that, they will wrap themselves around the blender blade.

2 pounds tomatillos (about 25 medium tomatillos)

8 serrano peppers

½ cup fresh lime juice (from about 4 medium limes)

2 cups yellow onion

8 garlic cloves

4 tablespoons extra virgin olive oil

6 cloves

2 cinnamon sticks

2 star anise pods

1 teaspoon cumin seeds

1 teaspoon coriander seeds

½ teaspoon mustard seeds

4-inch piece ginger, peeled, finely minced

2 tablespoons kosher salt, divided

2 cups diced roasted fennel stalk (reserved from Pickled Roasted Fennel Bulb, page 151)

1 cup rice vinegar

Makes 6 half-pints

Assemble the canning stations as described on pages 5–7, steps 2–4. At the food preparation station, soak the tomatillos in cold water for 10 minutes. Remove the husks and cores and compost them. Wash off the sticky residue from the tomatillos with warm water. Cut into large chunks. Wash the serranos under cold water and remove their stems. Juice the limes and set the juice aside. Peel the onion and garlic; dice the onion.

In a large, nonreactive saucepan, place the olive oil and cook over medium-high heat until the oil is fluid and hot. Add the cloves, cinnamon sticks, star anise, cumin seeds, coriander, and mustard seeds. When the spices start to bubble and pop, move the pan off the heat for 2 minutes to infuse the flavors into the oil. After 2 minutes, move the pan back to the heat and add the onions, garlic, ginger, and 1 tablespoon salt. Let the onions, garlic, and ginger fry in the oil, stirring only to avoid sticking, about 4 minutes. With metal tongs, remove the cinnamon stick, star anise pods, and cloves.

Add the fennel stalk, tomatillos, serranos, the remaining 1 tablespoon of salt, and the rice vinegar. Let simmer and reduce for 10 minutes. Add the lime juice to the sauce and turn off the heat. Using either an immersion blender or standing blender, blend the sauce until completely smooth. Return to the heat over a low simmer. Taste the sauce to ensure that it is properly seasoned.

At the filling station, fill the jars with curry sauce, leaving ½ inch of headspace. Remove the air pockets, wipe the rim, and secure the lid. Place the jars in the water bath, covered by 1 inch of water. Once the water is boiling, process for 10 minutes (pages 11–14, steps 7–12).

Preserved

FENNEL FROND CHIMICHURRI

While recipe-testing for one of my hot sauces, I found myself surrounded by lots of fennel. I was only using the bulbs, so I had a plethora of fronds to experiment with. This chimichurri was born out of that experimentation and is perfect for topping grilled meats and fish. The fennel adds a light licorice note that pairs nicely with the briny capers. (See photo on page 154.)

4 cups fennel fronds, loosely packed (reserved from Pickled Roasted Fennel Bulb, page 151)

½ cup flat-leaf parsley, loosely packed

¼ cup white balsamic vinegar

2 garlic cloves, peeled

1 tablespoon fresh lemon juice

1 teaspoon kosher salt

1 tablespoon capers, drained

½ teaspoon crushed red pepper flakes

¾ cup extra virgin olive oil

Makes 1½ cups

At the food preparation station, wash the fennel fronds and parsley under cold running water. Pull off the small light fronds by running your fingers down each stalk away from the bulb, to collect the fronds. Compost any brown or squishy fronds.

Pour white balsamic vinegar into a food processor. Add the garlic, fennel fronds, and parsley. Secure the lid and pulse 15 times, then scrape down the mixture with a rubber spatula. Add the lemon juice, salt, capers, and red pepper flakes. Pulse 15 more times, then scrape down the sides again. Secure the lid, pulse 10 more times, and scrape. Secure the lid, turn the processor on low, and slowly drizzle in about half the olive oil through the top. Stop the processor, remove the lid, scrape down the sides, secure the lid, turn on the processor, and drizzle in the remaining olive oil until well blended and all the ingredients are uniform, creating a smooth sauce, resembling a pesto.

Store in the refrigerator for up to 5 days or freeze for up to 1 year.

TIP
Use this chimichurri for the Scallops with Chimichurri recipe (page 155).

Fennel Frond Chimichurri, page 153.

Recipe

SCALLOPS WITH CHIMICHURRI

From cozy date nights to big family birthday parties, this is my go-to celebration meal. It is simple and special and the pairing of scallops with chimichurri makes for a killer combination. The key to cooking scallops well is to use a good pan and to get the pan super-hot before you add the seafood; that way, you will cook the scallops quickly, allowing them to crisp up and form a lovely crust. The finishing touch of the bright, fresh chimichurri really pushes this dish from ordinary to extraordinary.

15 large dry scallops

2 tablespoons extra virgin olive oil, plus more to drizzle

Salt and pepper, to taste

2 tablespoons salted butter

1 pint jar Pickled Roasted Fennel Bulb (page 151)

1 cup Fennel Frond Chimichurri (page 153)

Makes 2 servings

Pat scallop dry with a paper towel. Drizzle each side with a little olive oil and sprinkle with a little salt and pepper.

Heat 2 tablespoons olive oil in a medium skillet over medium-high heat. The oil should coat the entire bottom of the pan; if you're using a larger pan, add more oil if needed. When the oil is shimmering and fluid, add the butter. When the butter begins to melt and bubble, place the scallops in the pan 1 inch apart. Press lightly with a spatula to create even contact.

Let the scallops crisp by not moving or touching them for 2 minutes. After 2 minutes, carefully flip them using a flat spatula; if the scallops do not release easily, they are not ready to flip. Once the scallops are flipped, tilt the pan and let the liquid gather at the base. Use a spoon to baste the scallops. Continue basting for 1 minute. Set the pan flat on the burner and cook for 1 minute.

Lay down slices of the Pickled Roasted Fennel Bulb on a serving plate. Place the scallops on top of the fennel and drizzle with Fennel Frond Chimichurri.

TIP

It takes a bit of practice to get used to cooking at high temperatures. Try it first with one scallop to get the hang of it.

Nettles

Often called "stinging nettles," these Cascade natives can add excitement and danger to your canning agenda. The small, hairlike fibers along the leaves and stalk add a bit of a thrill to the kitchen experience—if touched, the follicles break and release formic acid that itches and irritates the skin. Even though nettles have a reputation for causing pain, they are also known for reducing allergy symptoms because of their anti-inflammatory qualities. Once these spiny culprits are blanched, they are more than safe to handle. Historically used to make a medicinal tea, nettles are wonderful culinary ingredients.

Canned

SPICY PICKLED GREENS

This is a northwest vegetarian spin on southern collard greens. Spicy, slightly smoky, and packed with flavor, this recipe is the ideal accompaniment to a big bowl of polenta. Nettles thrive in the Pacific Northwest and this dish is the perfect use for these stinging little gems. Once nettles are boiled, they are safe to handle, but prior to cooking them be careful by wearing long sleeves and rubber gloves.

8 ounces nettle leaves and stems

6 Thai chilies

2 medium shallots

1 teaspoon kosher salt

2½ cups plus 2 tablespoons red wine vinegar, divided

1½ cups dry red wine

1 tablespoon light brown sugar, packed

1 tablespoon yellow mustard seeds

1 teaspoon celery seeds

1 teaspoon Spanish smoked paprika

¼ teaspoon ground black pepper

3 ounces kale

Makes 6 half-pints

Assemble the canning stations as described on pages 5–7, steps 2–4. At the food preparation station, put on gloves and wash the nettles. Cut the stems into 4-inch pieces. Wash the Thai chilies, remove their tops, and leave the seeds. Peel and finely dice the shallots.

In a medium saucepan, bring 4 cups of water to a boil over high heat. Add the nettles, reduce the heat, and cover; let simmer for 40 minutes. Turn the heat off, add the salt and stir; let sit for 5 minutes. Line a colander with a double layer of cheesecloth and strain the liquid (vegetable rennet) into a bowl, saving it for the Nettle Ricotta Cheese recipe on page 160. When the nettles are cool to the touch, roll the leaves into a log and run a knife through it, slicing the greens into 1-inch ribbons.

In a large, nonreactive pot, sauté the shallots and 2 tablespoons vinegar until soft, about 3 minutes. Add the remaining 2 ½ cups vinegar, wine, brown sugar, and spices. Bring the brine to a boil over high heat. Once hot and bubbly, turn the heat down to low. Add the nettles and kale and stir together.

At the filling station, keep the jars and brine hot while filling each jar. Add a Thai chili to the bottom of the jar. With a slotted spoon and a funnel, pack the contents into the jar, leaving 1 inch of headspace. Use a heat-resistant pitcher to fill the jar with brine, leaving ½ inch of headspace. Remove the air pockets, add brine if necessary, wipe the rim, and secure the lid. Place the jars in the water bath, covered by 1 inch of water. Once the water is boiling, process for 10 minutes (pages 11–14, steps 7–12).

Ball

Canned

LEMON SPRING GREEN SAUCE

After taking a holiday break, we start the farmers' market again in the spring. By that point, I have missed my farm friends so much that I go to each of their stands to say hello, give hugs, and gather an array of greens. The leeks in this recipe provide a silky texture that pairs well with butter or cream sauces. In the summer when I don't want to turn on my oven, I open a jar of this sauce, heat it in a skillet with butter, and toss with my favorite pasta.

1 pound leeks (from 2 large leeks)

2 cups (1 ounce) fresh nettles

4 cups kale

6 medium garlic cloves

6 green jalapeños

1 sweet onion (about 2 cups chopped)

2 tablespoons plus 2 cups white balsamic vinegar

1 cup fresh lemon juice (from 5 large lemons)

2 tablespoons kosher salt

1 tablespoon local honey

Makes 6 half-pints

Assemble the canning stations as described on pages 5–7, steps 2–4. At the food preparation station, fill a medium bowl half-full with cold water. Chop the root end and the tough green top off the leeks and compost them, or freeze for future vegetable stock. Chop the leeks into ¼-inch rings and place in the water; run your hand through the leeks to separate the rings and loosen dirt from inside the leeks. Set this bowl aside.

Wearing gloves and long sleeves, wash the nettles and trim the nettle leaves from the stalk and stems. Wash the kale under cold running water. Trim off the stalks from the kale and set aside for the Romanesco Leaf Sauerkraut recipe on page 129. Roughly chop the kale and nettles into ½-inch strips. Peel the garlic and roughly chop. Wash the jalapeños under cold running water. Chop the tops off the jalapeños, split the peppers down the middle, from top to bottom, and remove their seeds. Peel the onion and roughly chop. Scoop the leeks out of the bowl of water with a slotted spoon and rinse under cold water.

In a medium, nonreactive saucepan over medium heat, place 2 tablespoons white balsamic vinegar, leeks, sweet onion, garlic, and jalapeños, and sauté until soft, about 6 minutes. Add the remaining 2 cups of white balsamic vinegar, lemon juice, salt, and honey and bring to a boil over medium-high heat. Once boiling, stir in the nettles and kale to wilt. Turn the heat to a low simmer and let the mixture reduce for 10 minutes.

Blend with an immersion blender until no large chunks remain.

At the filling station, keep the jars and sauce hot while filling each jar. Use a funnel and a heat-resistant pitcher, leaving ½ inch of headspace. Remove the air pockets, wipe the rim, and secure the lid. Place the jars in the water bath, covered by 1 inch of water. Once the water is boiling, process for 10 minutes (pages 11–14, steps 7–12).

TIP

You can use this sauce to make the Baked Nettle Cannelloni (page 162).

Preserved

NETTLE RICOTTA CHEESE

Nettles contain a coagulating enzyme similar to that found in animal rennet. By boiling the nettles in the Spicy Pickled Greens (page 157), you are creating a natural vegetable rennet that most people would discard. With the help of vinegar and whole milk, it is quite easy to create a creamy, chunky curd. The vegetable rennet is dark green in color so the blanched nettles help to enhance the visual appeal. This cheese makes a terrific spread for sandwiches or as an addition to a cheese plate.

2 fresh nettle leaves

3 cups non-ultrapasteurized whole milk

1 cup non-ultrapasteurized, heavy whipping cream

1 tablespoon distilled vinegar

1 tablespoon nettle rennet (reserved from Spicy Pickled Greens, page 157)

1 teaspoon kosher salt

Makes 1½ cups

Wearing rubber gloves and long sleeves, trim the nettle leaves from the stems with kitchen shears and set aside.

In a medium, heavy-bottom pot over medium heat, heat the whole milk and heavy whipping cream, stirring occasionally for about 10 minutes, until the milk reaches 190°F on a thermometer. Stir in the vinegar and rennet and bring the temperature back up to 190°F, about 2 minutes. Let sit for 15 minutes.

Meanwhile, prepare an ice-water bath in a medium bowl with 3 cups of water and 6 ice cubes. In a medium pot, boil 4 cups of water; blanch the nettle leaves in the water for 2 minutes, then remove them with tongs and place them into the ice-water bath. Pull out the nettles, dry them on a kitchen towel, and chiffonade, separating the pieces with your fingers.

Make a double lining of cheesecloth and place it in a fine-mesh strainer, inside a bowl. Pour the liquid through the cheesecloth, followed by the curds. Sprinkle the salt and nettles over the curds and fold together. Drain for 2 minutes, squeezing out any excess liquid. Serve warm or store in a glass container. Refrigerate for up to 5 days.

TIPS

Be sure to use fresh non-ultrapasteurized milk; otherwise, the curds will not form.

Save the whey that drains off the cheese to use in smoothies.

Use this ricotta for the Baked Nettle Cannelloni on page 162.

Recipe

BAKED NETTLE CANNELLONI

Baked pasta dishes may be heavy; however, the acidity level in the Lemon Spring Green Sauce lightens up this dish and brings a touch of bright, fresh spring to your winter meal. Although it is canned, it still tastes fresh and lively. This dish has become our quick weeknight meal to make together. My daughter loves mixing, so I ask her to stir the cheese and pipe it into the tubes, while my husband shreds the cheese.

1 pint Lemon Spring Green Sauce (page 157), divided

1 cup Nettle Ricotta Cheese (page 160)

1 cup whipping cream

2 four-ounce mozzarella balls, shredded, divided

¼ cup freshly grated Parmigiano-Reggiano

1 egg

Salt and pepper, to taste

14 cannelloni tubes

10 fresh basil leaves, chiffonade

Makes 2 servings

Preheat the oven to 350°F.

In a 4-quart glass baking dish, spread ½ cup Lemon Spring Green Sauce on the bottom of the dish.

In a medium bowl, stir together the ricotta, 1 cup whipping cream, ½ cup shredded mozzarella cheese, Parmigiano-Reggiano, and egg, and season with salt and pepper. Place the mixture into a piping bag or a plastic bag with the corner cut off. Place the dry cannelloni standing up inside a bowl and pipe the cheese mixture into each cannelloni tube. Continue filling the tubes until all are filled.

Lay the tubes in the sauce-lined baking dish. Pour the remaining sauce over the dish. Top with the remaining shredded mozzarella cheese and season with more salt and pepper. Cover with foil and bake for 25 to 30 minutes. Remove the foil and bake another 10 minutes, until golden brown and bubbling. Remove from the oven and let stand for 5 minutes. Garnish with fresh basil.

TIPS

If you did not make the Nettle Ricotta Cheese, replace with store-bought ricotta and 1 teaspoon of shredded fresh basil.

If you did not make the Lemon Spring Green Sauce, replace with a jar of sauce of your choosing.

For cannelloni recommendation, see Stocking Your Pantry on page 212.

Onions

Onions are loaded with vitamin C, folic acid, and sulfur, and have great benefits when incorporated into our diet. The intense sting of fresh onions is not for everyone; however, pickling, roasting, and caramelizing onions help to break down the sharp bite. Groundwork Organics is a local farm in Junction City, Oregon, and Matthew, one of the farmers, works year-round to preserve and can anything that is not purchased by restaurants or farmers' market shoppers. Most impressive are his powders in a rainbow of colors and flavors, including allium, shallot, spring sweet onion, and green garlic. The onion skin powder in this chapter is inspired by his food waste prevention efforts.

Canned

COFFEE BRAISED ONION JAM

Making caramelized onions takes a good amount of time and patience, but is always worth the wait. Having these onions on hand in the pantry enhances any soup, stew, or cheese board. While the onions braise in the oven, I encourage you to make other things in the kitchen. I usually have sauce bubbling away on the stovetop while my kitchen fills with the perfume of cooked onions.

2 cups French press coffee

2 heads of garlic

6 medium yellow onions

1 tablespoon olive oil

1½ tablespoons kosher salt, divided

½ cup balsamic vinegar

2 cups apple cider vinegar

1 teaspoon cayenne pepper

⅓ cup molasses

Makes 6 half-pints

Assemble the canning stations as described on pages 5–7, steps 2–4. Brew the coffee using a French press and a coarse grind. At the food preparation station, peel the garlic. Peel the onions, saving the skins for the Onion Peel Powder recipe on page 166. Cut the onions in half.

Preheat the oven to 350°F.

In a Dutch oven (or a heavy-bottom, oven-safe pot with a lid), place the olive oil. Over medium-high heat, add the onions cut-side down and leave them untouched for 4 minutes. After 4 minutes, flip the onions. Add the garlic, coffee, 1 tablespoon salt, balsamic vinegar, apple cider vinegar, and cayenne pepper.

Place the covered pot into the oven. Leave the pot closed and cook for 3 hours. Remove from the oven and add the molasses and the remaining ½ tablespoon salt. Using an immersion blender, blend until slightly chunky, with no large pieces.

At the filling station, keep the jam and jars hot while filling each jar. Use a funnel and a heat-resistant pitcher to fill the jars, leaving ½ inch of headspace. Remove the air pockets, wipe the rim, and secure the lid. Place the jars in the water bath, covered by 1 inch of water. Once the water is boiling, process for 10 minutes (pages 11–14, steps 7–12).

TIP

Use a dark-roast coffee for this recipe (see Stocking Your Pantry on page 212 for suggestions).

Canned

PINK PICKLED SHALLOTS

Although shallots are technically different from onions, they are both in the allium family and therefore in this shared chapter. These beauties are a spectacular tribute to all things pink. As the shallots infuse with the red wine vinegar and dance with the pink wine, the peppercorns round everything out with a nice bite. These shallots make the perfect addition to a grilled cheese sandwich or burgers, and the recipe has very little prep involved; just a quick peel and slice and you are ready to can.

1½ pounds shallots

2½ cups red wine vinegar

1½ cups dry rosé

1 tablespoon kosher salt

1 teaspoon pink peppercorns

8 sprigs fresh thyme, divided

Makes 6 half-pints

Assemble the canning stations as described on pages 5–7, steps 2–4. At the food preparation station, peel the skin off the shallots, rinse off any dirt, and cut into ¼-inch whole thin slices; separate the rings with your fingers.

In a medium, heavy-bottom saucepan, add the red wine vinegar, rosé, ½ cup of water, salt, peppercorns, and 2 sprigs thyme, and bring to a boil over high heat. Lower the heat to a bubbling simmer and let the brine infuse for 5 minutes, stirring occasionally. Turn the heat to the lowest setting.

(CONTINUED)

(CONTINUED)

At the filling station, keep the jars and brine hot while packing each jar. Strain the brine through a fine-mesh strainer into a heat-resistant pitcher and put the peppercorns in a bowl. Remove the hot jar from the pot, place a few peppercorns into the bottom of the jar, and pack with sliced shallots, packing them down with the back of a spoon; stop midway to add a sprig of thyme against the glass. Continue packing with shallots, leaving 1 inch of headspace. Use a funnel and fill each jar with brine, leaving ½ inch of headspace. Remove the air pockets by tapping the jars gently, add more brine if shallots are uncovered, wipe the rim, and secure the lid. Place the jars in the water bath, covered by 1 inch of water. Once the water is boiling, process for 10 minutes (pages 11–14, steps 7–12).

Preserved

ONION PEEL POWDER

Depending on the season, we can process up to 200 pounds of onions a week, which you can imagine leaves us with a huge quantity of onion skins! I used them in vegetable stocks and for my canning classes, but I was still left with buckets of onion waste. I decided to read up on the health benefits of onions and discovered that they actually store lots of antioxidants in their skins. The skins add a slight onion flavor and can also be substituted as a gluten-free alternative to asafoetida, a dried root with a sharp flavor that is used in Indian cooking.

4 cups yellow onion skins, loosely packed (from about 5 medium onions; reserved from Coffee Braised Onion Jam, page 165)

Makes 3 tablespoons

Separate each layer and get rid of any layers with spots. Place the skins in a bowl and cover with cold water. Let sit for 10 minutes and then drain. Rinse the skins under cold water, removing any stuck-on particles. Return to the bowl, cover with cold water, and let sit another 10 minutes. Drain the water and rinse the skins again. Compost any skins with dirt, spots, flesh of the onion, or multiple layers that will not come apart. Lay the skins between 2 tea towels and pat dry. Arrange on a drying rack, without the skins touching. Let air-dry for 48 hours, or dry in the oven at 150°F for 3 hours.

Once the skins are completely dry, crumble them by hand into a dry blender. Secure the lid and lay a towel over the top of the lid to collect any onion dust. Turn the blender on high and let it run for 5 minutes, until the onion skins are powdered. Store in an airtight jar out of direct sunlight for up to 6 months.

TIPS

Make sure the skins are very clean and dry. Moisture and dirt are enemies if you want to keep this powder in your pantry.

This same technique also works for shallots.

See Stocking Your Pantry on page 212 for blender recommendation.

small batch jams
Red Berries
small batch jams
Four Berry
GROUNDWORK
Strawberry

Recipe

CHEESE AND ONION BISCUITS

These are the perfect biscuits to take on a picnic or to a potluck. You can stuff them full of ham or partner them with fried chicken. They are quick, easy, and great to eat hot or cold—and they're cute as a button. The onion skins add antioxidants, which compensates for the decadent butter and cheese! If you didn't make the Onion Peel Powder (page 166), you can substitute with 1 teaspoon of store-bought onion powder.

2 cups all-purpose flour

1 tablespoon baking powder

1 tablespoon Onion Peel Powder (page 166)

½ teaspoon kosher salt

¼ teaspoon cayenne powder

1 cup buttermilk

1 egg

½ cup butter, room temperature

1 garlic clove, finely minced

1½ cups extra sharp cheddar cheese, shredded

Makes 24 mini biscuits

Preheat the oven to 450°F.

Place silicone baking mats onto two 12 x 16 baking sheets.

In a large bowl, combine the flour, baking powder, Onion Peel Powder, salt, and cayenne with a whisk.

In a separate bowl (or using a stand mixer), whisk the buttermilk, egg, butter, and garlic. Scrape down the bowl and beaters. Add the dry ingredients half a cup at a time. Then fold in the cheese with a rubber spatula.

Use a 1-inch ice cream scoop with a trigger to scoop the batter into balls on the mats.

Bake in the oven for 10 minutes, until golden brown. Serve immediately.

TIP

Whenever I refer to "shredded cheese," I am always referring to cheese that you shred yourself by hand. Store-bought shredded cheese has added ingredients that keep it from melting.

Recipe

FRENCH ONION SOUP

This classic soup can be made in minutes using the Coffee Braised Onion Jam (page 165) you so lovingly took all that time to make. Traditionally, this soup is made with beef bone broth, but you can substitute with the broth or stock of your choice. The soup is a bit more acidic than traditional French onion soup, which justifies all the cheese you are going to top it with!

4 tablespoons salted butter

4 tablespoons unbleached flour

4 cups stock (beef or vegetable)

1 half-pint Coffee Braised Onion Jam (page 165)

1 baguette

1 cup shredded Gruyère cheese, divided

1 sprig thyme

Makes 4 servings

Preheat the oven to 350°F.

In a large saucepan over medium heat, melt the butter. Once the butter is melted, whisk in the flour. After 2 minutes of whisking, pour in the stock. Bring to a boil over high heat and add the Coffee Braised Onion Jam. Turn the heat to low and let simmer, bubbling slightly for 5 minutes.

Slice the baguette into ¼-inch diagonal slices. Place the slices on parchment paper and top with ½ cup shredded cheese. Place in the oven for 5 minutes, until the cheese is melted.

Pour the soup into four bowls and top with the toasted cheese baguette. Garnish with the remaining ½ cup cheese and fresh thyme.

TIP

If you did not make the Coffee Braised Onion Jam, you can substitute with two large sliced onions, cooked until caramelized, about 45 minutes. Make sure to deglaze the pan with coffee as they cook.

Peppers

Peppers are one of my favorite ingredients to work with because of their health benefits and flavor profiles. With their low calories and ability to increase metabolic activity, in turn, resulting in burned calories and fat, peppers are part of my daily routine. There are many varieties and inspiring ways to use them. My favorite types are habañeros, serranos, and jalapeños. Each variety has a different strength and different attributes that can be highlighted with other fruits and vegetables. This chapter will demonstrate how to work with the natural heat and highlight the flavor, resulting in food packed full of beta-carotene, antioxidants, and the lively capsaicin.

Canned

CHERRY BOMB HOT SAUCE

Summer in Portland is short, beautiful, and prime time for peppers. Over the years, farmers in Oregon have started growing more and more of them, as more and more shoppers put them in their carts. But when we first started the market, we could only find a few types and so worked with farmers to grow the special varieties we were looking for. Cherry bomb peppers were one of those hard-to-find types; with their mild heat and thick walls, they are perfect for sauce making. This hot sauce is one of our favorites.

1 medium garlic head

3 medium yellow onions (about 4 cups)

2 cups distilled vinegar

3 pounds red tomatoes

2½ pounds cherry bomb peppers

3 tablespoons kosher salt

1 cup fresh lemon juice (from about 7 medium lemons)

3 tablespoons blue agave syrup

Makes 6 pints

Assemble the canning stations as described on pages 5–7, steps 2–4. At the food preparation station, peel the garlic and onions, saving the onion peels for the Onion Peel Powder recipe on page 166. Cut the onions into four quarters, and place the onions and garlic in a food processor; run until fine, about 3 minutes. If the ingredients get stuck, open the food processor, add a tablespoon of vinegar, and scrape down the sides with a rubber spatula.

In a large, stainless steel saucepan, place the vinegar and onion mixture. Heat on medium-high for 10 minutes, uncovered. Stir frequently to avoid sticking. Turn the heat down to the lowest setting and let simmer.

Meanwhile, wash the tomatoes and peppers under cold running water. Core the tomatoes and cut each one into four quarters; set aside. Use a paring knife to cut the tops off the peppers and scrape out the seeds and pith. Save the tops and seeds for the Chili Flake–Infused Sea Salt recipe on page 174.

In batches, put roughly equal parts tomatoes and peppers into a food processor and blend until smooth. Add the tomato-pepper mixture to the cooking onions and continue to sauté, and reduce for 25 minutes over medium-high heat. Add salt, lemon juice, and agave and continue stirring for 5 minutes.

At the filling station, keep the jars and sauce hot while filling each jar. Pour the sauce into a heat-resistant pitcher. Use a funnel and pour the sauce into the jars, leaving ½ inch of headspace. Remove the air pockets, wipe the rim, and secure the lid. Place the jars in the water bath, covered by 1 inch of water. Once the water is boiling, process for 10 minutes (pages 11–14, steps 7–12).

TIPS

If you want your hot sauce to be silky-smooth, you can process it in a blender before filling the jars.

This is a very mild hot sauce. If you want to make it spicy, substitute a hotter red pepper such as red serranos, red fresnos, or red jalapeños.

Canned

PICKLED PADRÓN PEPPERS

This is the simplest way to let these short-season Spanish peppers shine. While best known for being fried or grilled, this pickled version can be easily saved to enjoy later in the year. These mild peppers are the perfect replacement for pepperoncini for your salads and sandwiches. Or, serve the pickled bite as an appetizer wrapped in your favorite cured meat.

2 pounds Padrón peppers

6 medium garlic cloves

4 cups rice vinegar

2 bay leaves

1 teaspoon coriander

2 tablespoons kosher salt

30 whole peppercorns

Makes 6 pints

Assemble the canning stations as described on pages 5–7, steps 2–4. At the food preparation station, wash the peppers under cold running water. Leave the stems on or trim at the base, if desired. Cut 2 slits in each pepper vertically by inserting a paring knife into the pepper through the middle and into the other side, drawing the blade down; this will keep the peppers from floating. Peel the garlic.

In a large, nonreactive saucepan, combine vinegar, 3 cups of water, bay leaves, coriander, and salt. Bring the brine to a boil over high heat. Once hot and bubbly, turn the heat down to low.

At the filling station, keep the jars and brine hot while filling each jar. Place one garlic clove and five peppercorns into each jar. Pack each jar tightly with peppers, placing them stem-side up and then stem-side down to fill in the gaps, leaving 1 inch of headspace. Use a heat-resistant pitcher to fill the jar with brine, leaving ½ inch of headspace. Remove the air pockets by gently tapping the jars on a kitchen towel, add brine if necessary, wipe the rim, and secure the lid. Place the jars in the water bath, covered by 1 inch of water. Once the water is boiling, process for 10 minutes (pages 11–14, steps 7–12).

Preserved

CHILI FLAKE–INFUSED SEA SALT

When I need to give someone a special gift, I often make infused salts. They are quick and easy and last for quite some time. We usually have a huge amount of pepper tops on hand, resulting in copious amounts of spicy infused salt. I have made Chili Flake–Infused Sea Salt for dinner party gifts and for the holidays. This salt is also a great garnish for avocado toast.

20 pepper tops and seeds (reserved from Cherry Bomb Hot Sauce, page 173)

2½ cups coarse sea salt

Makes 6 quarter-pints

Preheat the oven to 200°F.

Place the pepper tops and seeds on a parchment paper–lined baking sheet. Place in the oven on the center rack. If you're using a gas oven, leave the door closed; if you're drying in an electric oven, prop the door open so moisture can escape. Check the peppers every 30 minutes, until there is still color but no moisture, about 1 to 3 hours. Remove the baking sheet from the oven and let cool.

Put the salt into a glass quart jar with a lid. Pop the stems off the pepper tops and compost the stems. Place the dried tops and seeds into a spice grinder and grind until chili flakes appear. Place the chili flakes into the jar of salt. Put a lid and band on and shake. Store in a cool, dry place; turn and shake the jar nightly for 1 week to infuse the pepper flavor into the salt.
(CONTINUED)

(CONTINUED)

Once complete, portion into small jars for easy trading or gift giving. Store in a cool, dry, dark place for up to 1 year.

TIPS

If you don't want to wait a week, you can grind the salt and dried pepper tops and stems in a spice grinder to quickly infuse the two.

If you didn't roast and dry the pepper tops, use 3 tablespoons of chili flakes instead.

Recipe

RED PORK POSOLE WITH BEER

We spend fall and winter working outside at the farmers' market and it gets cold in Portland. To warm us up after a long day, we eat lots of spicy soups and stews. Posole is a hearty Mexican stew that contains hominy, a puffed corn kernel. This recipe has a fun Pacific Northwest twist with the addition of IPA, a style of beer we are famous for.

2 cups beer (recommendation IPA)

2 cups Liquid Gold Vegetable Stock (page 52)

1 pound pork loin

1 teaspoon kosher salt

1 tablespoon Mexican oregano

1 cup Cherry Bomb Hot Sauce (page 173)

1 cup Green Enchilada Sauce (page 47)

2 tomatos (about 1½ cups)

2 cups cooked hominy

1 bunch cilantro

4 radishes, sliced

8 corn tortillas

1 lime, cut into 4 wedges

Makes 4 servings

TIP

If you are looking for hominy at your local store, check the aisle with foods from Mexico. If you still can't find it, substitute with cooked garbanzo beans.

Preheat the oven to 350°F.

Place the beer and stock into a Dutch oven or a large roasting pan with a lid. Place the pork in the center of the pan and sprinkle with salt and oregano. Surround the pork with Cherry Bomb Hot Sauce, Green Enchilada Sauce, tomatoes, and hominy. Cover the pan with the lid and roast in the oven for 3 hours.

Remove the pan from the oven and shred the pork with two forks. Pour the soup into bowls. Garnish with cilantro and sliced radishes. Serve with tortillas and lime wedges.

TIPS

If you did not make the Liquid Gold Vegetable stock, substitute with any vegetable stock.

If you did not make the Cherry Bomb Hot Sauce, substitute with 1 cup of marinara sauce.

If you did not make the Green Enchilada Sauce, replace with your favorite enchilada sauce.

Radishes

These underground dwellers thrive in Portland's climate. With two long growing seasons, we see all kinds of classic varieties, such as the French breakfast, red king, white icicle, and the stunning watermelon radish. We also see Asian varieties like daikon and mammoth Sakurajima. All these radish types are full of fiber and magnesium, making them great to use in fresh applications and garnishes. In this chapter, I hope to inspire you to eat the often discarded radish leaves. Delicious fresh, they are also easy to dry and add a lovely peppery flavor to your dishes.

Canned

TAMARI PICKLED RADISH PODS AND GARLIC SCAPES

Radish pods grow off a radish plant when it starts to seed. They are tiny drops that extend off the tops of the plants. I like to pick them when they're at their smallest, because when they get big they can get a bit tough. Radishes have two growing seasons, and in the first round, when the radish plants go to seed, we also have garlic scapes in the garden. Garlic scapes can also be found at the markets in May and June and they give the radish pods a nice garlicky bite.

5 cups radish pods

2 cups garlic scapes

2 tablespoons white sesame seeds

3 cups rice vinegar

½ cup tamari

1 tablespoon kosher salt

1½ teaspoons crushed red pepper flakes, divided

Makes 6 pints

Assemble the canning stations as described on pages 5–7, steps 2–4. At the food preparation station, wash the radish pods and garlic scapes. Cut the scapes into 1-inch pieces.

In a large, dry saucepan over medium-high heat, toast the sesame seeds, shaking the pan every 15 seconds for 2 minutes, until the seeds are fragrant; then place the toasted seeds on a plate.

Place vinegar, 2 cups of water, tamari, and salt in the pot. Bring to a boil over high heat. Once it's boiling, turn the heat to a low simmer and add the pods and scapes. Let them infuse for 5 minutes.

At the filling station, keep the jars and brine hot while filling each jar. Place ¼ teaspoon crushed red pepper flakes and ½ teaspoon toasted sesame seeds into each jar. Using a slotted spoon, scoop the pods and scapes into each jar, leaving 1 inch of headspace. Top the jars with brine, leaving ½ inch of headspace, and pressing down any floating pods. Remove the air pockets, wipe the rim, and secure the lid. Place the jars in the water bath, covered by 1 inch of water. Once the water is boiling, process for 10 minutes (pages 11–14, steps 7–12).

TIP

You can find tamari at specialty grocery stores (see Stocking Your Pantry, page 212).

Canned

STRAWBERRY UME PLUM PICKLED RADISHES

Fair warning: These pickles are not for everyone—they are salty, spicy, and really funky. Radishes get a bit fragrant when heated and people tend to either love them or go running far away. In college I shared a floor and a kitchen with a student from South Korea; whenever we had a break, she would head home and come back with jars of funky fermented goodies, like kimchi and gochujang. The halls were instantly filled with a spicy-sweet fermenting essence and remembering it still makes my mouth water. When I make these pickles, I am immediately transported back in time. The ume plum vinegar is made from salted umeboshi plums and the fresh shiso leaf gives it a delicate edge.

5 bunches radishes (about 40 radishes)

4 cups rice vinegar

1 cup Strawberry Simple Syrup (right)

½ cup ume plum vinegar

8 shiso leaves, divided

1 tablespoon whole peppercorns

1 teaspoon crushed red pepper flakes

Makes 6 pints

Assemble the canning stations as described on pages 5–7, steps 2–4. At the food preparation station, wash the radishes under cold running water and trim the leaves, leaving ¼ inch; save the leaves for the Radish Top Za'atar recipe on page 183. Cut the radishes in half from stem to base, and in half again from stem to base.

In a large, nonreactive saucepan, place the rice vinegar, 2 cups of water, Strawberry Simple Syrup, ume plum vinegar, 2 shiso leaves, peppercorns, and crushed red pepper flakes. Bring to a boil over high heat. Once boiling, turn the heat to low and simmer; let infuse for 5 minutes. Using tongs, remove the 2 shiso leaves, and compost or consume.

At the filling station, keep the jars and brine hot while filling each jar. Lay a shiso leaf against the side of a jar, place the radishes in the jar, packing them in tightly and leaving 1 inch of headspace. Use a heat-resistant pitcher to fill the jar with brine, leaving ½ inch of headspace. Remove the air pockets, add brine if necessary, wipe the rim, and secure the lid. Place the jars in the water bath, covered by 1 inch of water. Once the water is boiling, process for 10 minutes (pages 11–14, steps 7–12).

TIP

You can purchase ume plum vinegar at specialty grocery or Asian markets (see Stocking Your Pantry on page 212).

Preserved

STRAWBERRY SIMPLE SYRUP

1 cup strawberries

1 cup granulated sugar, divided

¼ cup fresh lemon juice (from about 1 large lemon)

Makes 1 half-pint

Rinse the strawberries under cold running water and remove the strawberry tops, reserving for the Strawberry Top Salad Dressing on page 115. Smash the berries with a potato masher, sprinkle with ½ cup sugar, and let macerate for 10 minutes.

In a small skillet over medium heat, place the macerated strawberries, the remaining ½ cup sugar, and the lemon juice. Let cook until the strawberries begin to break down, about 5 minutes. Pour the mixture through a jelly bag and store in the refrigerator for up to 5 days.

TIP

Save the strawberry pulp to add to plain yogurt.

Canned

PICKLED RADISHES, CARROTS, AND JALAPEÑOS

Every time I make these pickles I am simultaneously planning our next taco/nacho/fajita party. I have also been known to eat a whole jar of them while setting up said party. If I don't can enough of these beauties to get me through winter, I visit my favorite taqueria, because I crave these pickled, spicy veggies. You can usually find me there standing over the toppings bar filling my bowl, not worried that my tacos are eight orders away.

15 radishes (about 2 cups sliced)

4 carrots (about 2 cups sliced)

6 jalapeños (about ¾ cup sliced)

4 cups distilled vinegar

2 tablespoons salt

1 tablespoon Mexican oregano

1 teaspoon whole dried cumin

6 whole garlic cloves

6 dried bay leaves

Makes 6 half-pints

Assemble the canning stations as described on pages 5–7, steps 2–4. At the food preparation station, wash the radishes, carrots, and jalapeños under cold running water and remove the stems. Slice the vegetables into ¼-inch coins.

In a medium saucepan over medium-high heat, cook the vinegar, 3 cups of water, salt, oregano, and cumin until it boils. Turn the heat down to medium and simmer uncovered for 5 minutes. Add the vegetables and garlic and cook for 3 minutes.

At the filling station, use a slotted spoon and funnel to ladle the vegetables into hot jars, filling half full. Tuck a bay leaf against the side of each jar, ensuring visibility. Fill the jars with vegetables, leaving 1 inch of headspace. Top the jars with brine, leaving ½ inch of headspace. Remove the air pockets, wipe the rim, and secure the lid. Place the jars in the water bath, covered by 1 inch of water. Once the water is boiling, process for 10 minutes (pages 11–14, steps 7–12).

TIP

If you are feeling adventurous, try adding 1 teaspoon dried epazote to the brine. Epazote is an herb used in South American dishes and tastes great.

Preserved

RADISH TOP ZA'ATAR

When I was a child, we had a pet bunny named Floppers. My mother kept a vegetable garden, which meant there was always plenty of food for him. He feasted on carrot tops, cabbage, and especially radish tops. When my grandmother came to visit, she was surprised that we gave these precious radish tops to our pet; she loved to add them to her soups and stews. My grandmother is my inspiration for this za'atar, often used in Middle Eastern dishes. The radish tops add an earthy, peppery depth to this spice blend.

TIP
If you do not have a salt block, you can use the oven or a food dehydrator to dry the tops, or if you do not have radish tops, or are pressed for time, substitute with 1 tablespoon of dried oregano.

8 large radish tops, dried and crumbled (about 2 tablespoons) (reserved from Strawberry Ume Plum Pickled Radishes page 180)

6 tablespoons sesame seeds

2 tablespoons kosher salt

4 tablespoons dried thyme

2 tablespoons sumac

Makes 4 quarter-pints

Gently rinse the radish tops under cold running water and trim off the stems. Fill a clean sink with 3 inches of cold water. Let the radish tops soak for 5 minutes. Remove the tops and pat dry between 2 paper towels. Arrange the tops on a salt block, close to each other but not touching. After 72 hours of drying, use the back of a butter knife to scrape the leaves off the salt block into a mortar and pestle.

In a dry saucepan over medium heat, toast the sesame seeds, shaking the pan from side to side to avoid burning. Once the seeds are slightly brown and begin to pop, take them off the heat and transfer to a dry bowl. Let cool.

Add salt to the radish tops and grind in the mortar and pestle until the tops are powdered. Add the cooled sesame seeds, thyme, and sumac, and grind until well mixed and fragrant. Store in a glass vessel in a cool, dark place for up to 6 months.

TIP
I often make one big batch of Radish Top Za'atar to give as summer barbecue gifts. It is really tasty melted with butter over corn or with olive oil on flatbread.

Recipe

BAKED LENTIL FALAFEL TACOS

I like to keep dried lentils and other pantry staples on hand. This recipe is easy, but it takes a little preplanning since you don't have to precook the lentils. Soaking the lentils the night before will ensure that you are on your way to a delicious Mediterranean lunch. The sesame sauce has a delicate texture from the yogurt and is one million times better than store-bought tahini.

FALAFELS

1 cup red lentils

1 bunch flat-leaf parsley (about 2 cups)

1 bunch cilantro (about 1 cup)

2 tablespoons Coffee Braised Onion Jam (page 165)

1 tablespoon Radish Top Za'atar (page 183)

2 tablespoons extra virgin olive oil

½ teaspoon baking soda

2 tablespoons garbanzo bean flour

SESAME DRESSING

1 cup hulled sesame seeds

3 garlic cloves, peeled

4 tablespoons plus ½ cup extra virgin olive oil, divided

1 teaspoon kosher salt

4 tablespoons fresh lemon juice

1 tablespoon pickling brine from 1 half-pint Pickled Radishes, Carrots, and Jalapeños (page 182)

1 teaspoon Radish Top Za'atar

¼ cup plain yogurt

Olive oil cooking spray

10 tortillas

½ head purple cabbage, shredded

½ head lettuce, shredded

1 half-pint Pickled Radishes Carrots, and Jalapeños (page 182)

Makes 4 servings

Place the lentils into a 32-ounce mason jar, cover with 2 cups of cold water, and let sit for 12 to 24 hours.

To make the falafel mixture, drain the lentils and pulse in a food processor 15 times, until rice-sized. Add in the parsley, cilantro, Coffee Braised Onion Jam, 1 tablespoon Radish Leaf Za'atar, and 2 tablespoons of olive oil. Blend until smooth and green, scraping down the sides with a rubber spatula as necessary. Place the mixture into a bowl and add the baking soda and garbanzo bean flour. Mix by hand. Refrigerate the mixture for 30 minutes.

Preheat the oven to 375°F.

Meanwhile, make the sesame dressing by toasting the sesame seeds in a medium skillet over medium heat, shaking the pan every 15 seconds, for 3 minutes, until golden brown. Immediately remove the seeds from the pan and put the seeds and garlic into the food processor; pulse 15 times, then add 1 tablespoon olive oil and pulse 5 times. With the processor on, slowly drizzle in 3 tablespoons of olive oil. Scrape down the sides. Turn processor back on and add the kosher salt, lemon juice, pickling brine, and yogurt. Drizzle in the remaining ½ cup olive oil. Run until smooth. Remove the mixture from the processor, pour into a small bowl, and sprinkle with 1 teaspoon za'atar. Set aside.

Line a baking sheet with parchment paper. Take out the falafel mixture from the refrigerator, roll into 1-inch balls, and place them on the baking sheet. Spray the falafels lightly with olive oil cooking spray. Place in the center rack of the oven and bake for 20 minutes, until hard to the touch and split slightly across the top.

Serve the falafels in warm tortillas and sprinkle evenly with the sesame dressing, shredded cabbage and lettuce, and pickled radishes, carrots, and jalapeños.

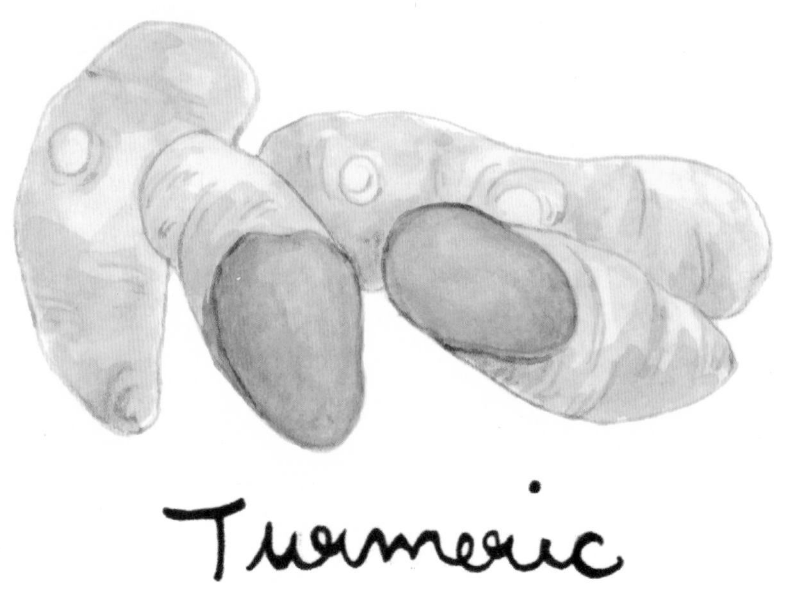

Turmeric

These neon-orange tubers can be spotted in our farmers' markets at a pretty penny. Keeping these roots warm in our cold, wet climate drives up the price, as turmeric can take ten months to cultivate and farmers often keep these plants in hothouses. They can also be grown in kitchen windows from small roots. Using fresh turmeric in cooking adds a lovely, pungent, peppery zing that is only outdone by its many health benefits. Since these roots are the powerhouse anti-inflammatory and antioxidant, I keep the skins in my freezer as my secret kitchen weapon for stocks and broths. In this chapter, I pass my secrets on to you. Caution: Working with turmeric can be a dangerous game. It will dye anything it comes into contact with, except stainless steel. If you process this in your blender, it will forever be yellow. Instead, use a stainless steel immersion blender or a food mill.

Turmeric Mustard, page 188.

Canned

TURMERIC MUSTARD

Fresh turmeric is a neon-orange underground dweller I like to call the "wonder root." It is said to be loaded with anti-inflammatory, antidepressant, and arthritis-management properties. Trust me, you need it in your life. When we first made an attempt to add turmeric to our daily routine, this mustard was our gateway. Now I sneak it into everything from salad dressings to sandwiches and even marinades. One of my other favorite ingredients to add to condiments and sauces is garbanzo bean flour. It is made from ground garbanzo beans and is a fantastic thickening agent. (See photo on page 187.)

4 medium garlic cloves

4 one-inch pieces fresh turmeric

2 cups white balsamic vinegar, divided

8 tablespoons yellow mustard powder

2 tablespoons kosher salt

4 tablespoons garbanzo bean flour

1 teaspoon sweet paprika

1 teaspoon onion powder

½ teaspoon turmeric powder

3 tablespoons local honey

Makes 6 quarter-pints

Assemble the canning stations as described on pages 5–7, steps 2–4. At the food preparation station, wear gloves to peel the garlic and turmeric, saving the turmeric peels for the Turmeric Skin Golden Cashew Milk (page 191) or the Liquid Gold Vegetable Stock (page 52).

Place 1 cup of white balsamic vinegar, the garlic cloves, and the fresh turmeric in a blender and blend on high until smooth. Set aside.

In a medium bowl, place the yellow mustard powder, kosher salt, garbanzo bean flour, sweet paprika, onion powder, and turmeric powder, and whisk to combine. Set aside.

Pour the blender mixture, the remaining 1 cup of white balsamic vinegar, and 2 cups of water into a large, nonreactive pot. Heat on high until boiling.

Turn the heat down to medium-high and begin whisking in the dry ingredients ¼ cup at a time, stirring frequently, and adding more dry ingredients once the powder is incorporated. Once all the dry ingredients are added, turn the heat to a low simmer and add the honey. Continue stirring occasionally to avoid sticking and cook for 10 to 15 minutes uncovered, until thickened. Turn the heat down to the lowest setting.

At the filling station, keep the jars and mustard hot while filling each jar. Ladle the mustard into a heat-resistant pitcher and use a funnel to fill each jar, leaving ¼ inch of headspace. Remove the air pockets, wipe the rim, and secure the lid. Place the jars in the water bath, covered by 1 inch of water. Once the water is boiling, process for 10 minutes (pages 11–14, steps 7–12).

TIPS

Look for fresh turmeric at the farmers' market in late summer. If you can't find it, try your local Asian grocery or natural food store. It is often in the produce section by the ginger or wrapped in packages. It is a small, dark-brown root.

Use this mustard to make the Cucumber Mustard Hot Sauce (page 142) and the Mustard Lime Sandwich Slicers (page 143).

Wear gloves and use caution when working with turmeric; it can stain counters, your skin, and clothes.

Canned

TURMERIC GINGER JUICE SHOTS

There are numerous benefits to juicing, clean eating, and health consciousness, but the busier I get, the less likely I am to think about healthy food choices. When I know I have a busy schedule coming up, I put aside a bit of time to whip up a batch of this juice. During the hustle and bustle, it brings a quick, healthy, energetic boost to my mornings. The ginger, cayenne pepper, and black pepper give this juice a nice tingle in the throat, while the honey and orange juice balance the spice with a light sweetness.

4 cups fresh orange juice (from about 15 medium oranges)

1 cup fresh lemon juice (from about 6 medium lemons)

1-inch piece ginger, peeled, minced

1-inch piece turmeric, peeled minced

1 tablespoon local honey

¼ teaspoon cayenne pepper

¼ teaspoon ground black pepper

Makes 15 (2-ounce) bottles

Assemble the canning stations as described on pages 5–7, steps 2–4. At the food preparation station, zest the oranges and the lemons, saving the zest for the Tomato Skin Togarashi recipe on page 104 and the Lemon Peel Spice Rub recipe on page 61. Once the zest has been removed, slice the fruit in half and juice. Wearing gloves, mince the ginger and turmeric.

Place the juice, ginger, turmeric, honey, cayenne pepper, and black pepper in a medium, nonreactive, stainless steel saucepan and bring the juice to a boil. Once boiling, turn the heat down to low and steep for 5 minutes.

Place the contents of the saucepan in a blender and blend for 3 minutes on high, until no peels or pulp are visible. Strain the contents of the blender through a jelly bag (retaining the foam) into a heat-resistant pitcher.

At the filling station, keep the jars and juice hot while filling each jar. Using a small funnel, fill the jar with juice, leaving ¼ inch of headspace. Wipe the rim and secure the lid. Place the jars in the water bath, covered by 1 inch of water. Once the water is boiling, process for 10 minutes (pages 11–14, steps 7–12).

TIP

Wear gloves and use caution when working with turmeric; it can stain counters, your skin, and clothes.

Preserved

TURMERIC SKIN GOLDEN CASHEW MILK

Named for its glowing golden color, traditionally, this "golden milk" is served right before bed. Sweet, spicy, and comforting, it makes you feel alive as you sip it. Ideal for clearing up head colds, it's also great for warming up on a cold, rainy day. I encourage you to try your hand at making your own nut milk just to taste how much better homemade can be, but feel free to use store-bought in a pinch. When making nut milks, it is important to let the nuts soak overnight, so plan ahead. You can also substitute your favorite nut; I myself often swap out cashews for hazelnuts or almonds.

1 cup raw unsalted cashews

¼ cup turmeric peels (reserved from Turmeric Mustard, page 188)

¼-inch piece ginger, skin on

1 teaspoon maple syrup

¼ teaspoon turmeric powder

¼ teaspoon cayenne pepper

2 grinds of black pepper

Makes 6 (4-ounce) servings

Place the nuts in a 32-ounce jar and cover with 1 cup of cold water. Let soak for 24 hours.

After soaking, drain off the water.

In a medium saucepan over high heat, bring 4 cups of water to a boil. Once boiling, turn off the heat and let stand for 4 minutes. Set aside.

Place the nuts, turmeric skins, ginger, maple syrup, turmeric powder, cayenne pepper, and black pepper in the blender. Pour in the hot water. Turn the blender on low and let run for 2 minutes.

Strain the mixture through a fine-mesh strainer, saving the pulp for the Turmeric Cashew Chocolate Chip Cookies (page 192).

Serve the golden milk warm in a mug or a tiny cup. Store any leftover milk in the refrigerator for up to 5 days.

TIPS

This milk can also be frozen in ice cube trays and added to smoothies.

Wear gloves and use caution when working with turmeric; it can stain counters, your skin, and clothes.

If you do not have saved turmeric paste, substitute whole, unpeeled turmeric root.

Recipe

TURMERIC CASHEW CHOCOLATE CHIP COOKIES

When my husband and I go to work at the farmers' market, my father takes our two-year-old daughter out for the day. I love to send them off on their adventures with homemade snacks. These cookies are toddler- and Grandpa-approved, and give them both plenty of energy for their day of play. Turmeric Cashew Chocolate Chip Cookies are simple, filling, and best eaten when they are warm and gooey. Finishing these off with Portland-based, large-crystal, Jacobsen sea salt makes them over-the-top delicious.

TIP
If you do not have strained nut pulp from the Turmeric Skin Golden Nut Milk, substitute with ¼ cup finely chopped cashews, 1 teaspoon vanilla, and ¼ teaspoon turmeric powder.

1 cup (2 sticks) salted butter, room temperature

1 cup light brown sugar, loosely packed

1 cup granulated sugar

2 eggs

4 tablespoons strained nut pulp (reserved from Turmeric Skin Golden Cashew Milk, page 191)

2 cups all-purpose unbleached flour

1 teaspoon baking soda

1 teaspoon baking powder

1 teaspoon kosher salt

2 cups quick-cooking rolled oats

Two 3.5-ounce chocolate bars

1 teaspoon large-flake sea salt (optional)

Makes 24 cookies

In a large stand mixer, cream the butter and sugars on medium speed until smooth, about 3 minutes. Add the eggs and nut pulp and mix for 5 minutes.

In a medium bowl, combine the flour, baking soda, baking powder, and salt. Set aside.

Continue mixing the ingredients in the stand mixer on medium speed and add the flour mixture half a cup at a time, until thoroughly combined. Continue mixing and add the oats one cup at a time, until combined.

Chop the chocolate bars into ¼-inch chunks. Stir in the chocolate pieces with a rubber spatula and mix thoroughly.

Portion the dough into 1-inch-diameter balls using a stainless steel ice cream scoop, or roll by hand. Place the balls on 2 parchment-lined baking sheet about 1½ inches apart. Refrigerate for 30 minutes.

After the first 15 minutes, preheat the oven to 350°F. After 30 minutes, place both sheets into the oven on separate racks. Bake for 7 minutes. Rotate the pans and bake for another 6 minutes, until golden brown. Remove the trays from the oven and sprinkle with sea salt, if desired.

TIP
This cookie dough freezes wonderfully! Put the formed cookies on a parchment-lined baking sheet and place them in the freezer; once frozen, store them in a container until you're ready to bake them.

Zucchini

When zucchinis are harvested early, they have a lower moisture content, which helps to highlight their delicate flavor. With their soft skin and small seeds, zucchinis also make for easy kitchen prep. They appear in the summer and we are inundated with an avalanche of all squash varieties. Zucchinis are packed full of vitamins A and C, while also containing a high proportion of omega-3 fatty acids, making them a healthy vegan fat source. We bake them in breads, make spreads and dips, and can't pickle them fast enough. We use the whole zucchini in these recipes, so there is no food waste. Instead, we explore preserving the zucchini blossoms for an extended winter shelf life.

TIP
You can use this recipe to garnish the Green Tomato Bloody Mary (page 44).

Canned

TINY DILL ZUCCHINI PICKLES

This recipe also works with regular-sized sliced or cubed zucchinis, but they are irresistibly cute when they are tiny. This particular recipe always gets me out into the garden right when my plant starts to produce so I can snatch up the first tiny crop. You can also use mini patty pan squash, which I like to mix in by stacking three of them against the side of the pint jar.

2½ pounds mini zucchinis

6 heads fresh dill

6 garlic cloves

2½ cups distilled vinegar

1½ cups apple cider vinegar

4 tablespoons kosher salt

1 tablespoon dill seeds

1 teaspoon peppercorns

1 tablespoon mustard seeds

Makes 6 pints

Assemble the canning stations as described on pages 5–7, steps 2–4. At the food preparation station, wash the zucchinis and dill under cold running water. Trim the dill heads from the stalk. Peel the garlic.

In a large, nonreactive saucepan, place the distilled vinegar, apple cider vinegar, 2 cups of water, salt, dill seeds, peppercorns, and mustard seeds. Bring to a boil until the salt is dissolved, about 5 minutes. Turn the heat down to low and let the brine infuse for 5 minutes.

At the filling station, keep the jars and brine hot while filling each jar. Pour the brine through a fine-mesh strainer into a heat-resistant pitcher. Spoon the spices into the bottom of each jar. Place 1 garlic clove and 1 head of dill against the side of each jar. Tightly pack each jar with mini zucchinis, leaving 1 inch of space from the top; trim the zucchinis, if needed. Use a heat-resistant pitcher and funnel to pour the brine into the jars, leaving ½ inch of headspace. Remove the air pockets, add brine if necessary, wipe the rim, and secure the lid. Place the jars in the water bath, covered by 1 inch of water. Once the water is boiling, process for 10 minutes (pages 11–14, steps 7–12).

TIPS

You can pack a fresh grape leaf into the jar to help keep the pickles crisp, although it sometimes brings a bitter note. Either place it against the side or fold it onto the top, submerged in the brine, which in turn keeps the pickles from floating.

This recipe is also perfect for making dill pickles; simply substitute pickling cucumbers for mini zucchinis and pack them into 3-quart jars.

Canned

ZUCCHINI AND CASHEW CRÈME SAUCE

If you have ever tried your hand at growing zucchinis, you know that when they come in, they come in big and plentiful. Exciting at the onset, the realization quickly sets in that one can only eat so many zucchini pickles and loaves of zucchini bread. This recipe came from a class I taught to zucchini gardeners facing such problems. It makes a wonderful sauce when tossed with pasta or you can heat it up with lots of grated Parmigiano cheese and enjoy it as a dip. I would scream my love from the hills for piment d'Espelette; these are dried ground chilies from the Basque region and they add a subtle smoky heat.

6 medium zucchinis (about 8 cups, cubed)

2 medium yellow onions (about 4 cups, chopped)

1 head roasted garlic

2 tablespoons plus 1 cup white balsamic vinegar, divided

1 teaspoon dried basil

½ teaspoon dried oregano

½ teaspoon piment d'Espelette

¼ cup unsalted cashews

1 tablespoon plus ½ teaspoon kosher salt

¾ cup fresh lemon juice (from about 4 lemons)

Makes 6 pints

Assemble the canning stations as described on pages 5–7, steps 2–4. At the food preparation station, wash the zucchinis under cold running water. Cut off the stem ends, and compost. Slice zucchinis into 1-inch chunks. Peel the onion and dice into 1-inch chunks. Remove the garlic cloves from the roasted head of garlic.

In a large, nonreactive saucepan over medium-high heat, cook 2 tablespoons vinegar. Add the onions, stirring occasionally for 5 minutes to avoid sticking. Add the zucchinis, garlic cloves, ½ cup vinegar, ½ cup of water, basil, oregano, and piment d'Espelette. Cover and cook for 10 minutes.

Meanwhile, grind the cashews and 1 tablespoon salt, using a mortar and pestle, until the mixture forms a smooth powder. Once the contents in the saucepan have cooked for 10 minutes, add the powder to the pot and stir for 2 minutes as the mixture bubbles. Pour in the lemon juice, the remaining ½ cup vinegar, and the remaining ½ teaspoon salt. Turn the heat down to low and stir to combine. Blend ingredients in the pot using an immersion blender until desired consistency. Let cook for 2 minutes, stirring occasionally, until the sauce settles.

TIP
Use this sauce to make the Zucchini Crème Orecchiette Pasta (page 203).

At the filling station, keep the jars and the sauce hot while filling each jar. Use a funnel and a heat-resistant pitcher to fill the jars, leaving ½ inch of headspace. Remove the air pockets, wipe the rim, and secure the lid. Place the jars in the water bath, covered by 1 inch of water. Once the water is boiling, process for 10 minutes (pages 11–14, steps 7–12).

TIPS

Look for piment d'Espelette in specialty grocery stores (or see Stocking Your Pantry on page 212). If you can't find it, substitute with ¼ teaspoon crushed red pepper flakes, finely ground.

This sauce has an acidic bite (post-canning), but that can be easily lessened by simmering it for a couple minutes with 4 tablespoons of butter, coconut milk, or heavy cream.

Canned

BREAD AND BUTTER ZUCCHINI PICKLES

My mother-in-law's pickles and jams make our family gatherings extra special. Spring and summer bring some of her busiest days, as they are filled with canning special treats for everyone she knows. These pickles are our daughter's favorite and she will eat the whole jar if we let her. This recipe is inspired by Grandma Devery's pickles; she traditionally uses cucumbers instead of zucchinis, but either one works great!

6 medium zucchinis (about 8 cups)

1 medium onion or 2 large shallots

6 garlic cloves

2 tablespoons kosher salt

4 cups apple cider vinegar

2 cups light brown sugar, loosely packed

2 tablespoons mustard seeds

1 tablespoon dill seeds

1 tablespoon celery seeds

1 tablespoon crushed red pepper flakes

1 teaspoon turmeric powder

Makes 6 pints

Assemble the canning stations as described on pages 5–7, steps 2–4. At the food preparation station, wash the zucchinis under cold running water. Cut off the blossom ends, and compost, or put into the freezer for future stock making. Thinly slice the zucchinis into ⅛-inch-thick coins. Slice the onion into ⅛-inch-thick rounds. Peel the garlic and thinly slice.

In a large bowl, combine the zucchini, salt, and 2 tablespoons of cold water. Gently rub the salt into the zucchini coins. Place the bowl with the coins in the refrigerator for 15 minutes.

In a medium saucepan, bring the vinegar to a boil. Once it's boiling, turn the heat down to low and add the brown sugar. Stir to dissolve.

After 15 minutes, drain the liquid out of the zucchini bowl, but do not rinse. Add the onions, garlic, and spices. Wearing gloves, massage the spices into the vegetables.

At the filling station, keep the jars and brine hot while filling each jar. Hand-pack the vegetables into the jar. Press the pickles down gently with a spoon, leaving 1 inch of headspace. Use a heat-resistant pitcher to fill the jar with brine, leaving ½ inch of headspace. Remove the air pockets by tapping the jar gently on a kitchen towel. Add brine, if necessary, press the pickles down with the back of a spoon, wipe the rim, and secure the lid. Place the jars in the water bath, covered by 1 inch of water. Once the water is boiling, process for 10 minutes (pages 11–14, steps 7–12).

TIP

Cutting the blossom end from both zucchini and cucumbers helps to keep the pickled vegetable crisp as the enzymes in the blossom end will soften the pickles more quickly.

Preserved

OVEN-DRIED SQUASH BLOSSOMS

Traditionally stuffed with cheese and then fried, squash blossoms begin to appear at the farmers' market in early spring and are often snatched up in the opening hour by morning shoppers. In my own garden, they would bloom and fade just as my zucchini came to life, so I started drying the flowers using a technique bakers use to preserve violets. Initially, I would paint each flower with a small brush (a very tedious process), as I had seen it done in France, but these blossoms are hearty and can stand up to a squeeze. The Chinese Five-Spice Powder brings a savory essence of fall to these spring jewels. Crunchy and spiced, these blossoms make a perfect snack or textural addition to any salad.

1 tablespoon fresh lemon juice

15 squash blossoms

½ cup granulated sugar

1½ teaspoons Chinese Five-Spice Powder (right)

3 egg whites

Makes 15 blossoms

Fill a medium bowl with cold water and the lemon juice and rinse the blossoms in the lemon water. Remove the water from the flowers by holding the stem end, shaking lightly, and tapping the blossom against the side of the bowl. Set the flowers on a cloth napkin to dry, cover with another napkin, and pat gently.

While the flowers are drying, place the sugar and Chinese Five-Spice Powder in a dry food processor. Run until the sugar is super-fine, creating a light powder.

Preheat the oven to 200°F. Line a large baking sheet with parchment paper.

In a medium bowl, beat the egg whites with a fork, until foamy, removing any clumps. Dip the blossoms into the egg whites, squeezing any excess off between 2 fingers and spreading the blossom out as you squeeze. The blossom should be coated but not dripping. Over a plate, dust the super-fine sugar evenly, covering all parts of the flower. Place the flowers on the baking sheet and put the sheet into the center of the oven. If you're using an electric oven, prop the door open to allow moisture to escape; if you're using a gas oven, shut the door. Check the blossoms every 30 minutes, for 2 to 3 hours; the flowers should be dry and crisp with no moisture. Do not take them out of the oven until they're crisp to the touch.

These flowers will keep in the pantry for up to 3 months in a container, uncovered.

TIPS

Take your time with this one. When you peek in the oven and it looks like all is amiss, keep calm; the sugar running off the flower is part of the candy process.

Save the egg yolks for making the Strawberry Top Salad Dressing on page 115.

CHINESE FIVE-SPICE POWDER

1 teaspoon ground cinnamon

1 teaspoon ground star anise

1 teaspoon fennel seeds

1 teaspoon whole Sichuan peppercorns

½ teaspoon ground cloves

Makes 2 teaspoons

Grind all the spices with a mortar and pestle or a spice grinder until fine.

Recipe

ZUCCHINI CRÈME ORECCHIETTE PASTA

The first time my husband and I made this dish, it was just pasta and sauce and it was lovely. However, the second time we made it, we added mushrooms and toasted breadcrumbs and it was fantastic. Feel free to add whatever seasonal vegetables you prefer and choose whichever pasta shape you enjoy. This recipe is simple and easy and doesn't make a huge mess.

¼ cup panko breadcrumbs

2 teaspoons kosher salt, divided

10 ounces orecchiette pasta

1 teaspoon olive oil

½ pound cremini mushrooms, thinly sliced

1 cup heavy whipping cream

1 half-pint Zucchini and Cashew Crème Sauce (page 198)

¼ cup grated Parmigiano-Reggiano cheese

¼ cup fresh basil, chiffonade

Makes 2 servings

In a large dry skillet, toast the breadcrumbs over medium heat, shaking the skillet every 15 seconds, for 3 minutes, until golden brown. Move the breadcrumbs to a small plate to stop them from cooking.

In a medium pot over high heat, bring 6 cups of water and 1 teaspoon salt to a boil. Once at a boil, add the orecchiette. Stir the pasta as it boils, to keep it from sticking; boil for 10 minutes.

In the large skillet over medium-high heat, cook the olive oil; once hot and shimmering, add the mushrooms, sautéing until the moisture cooks out and the mushrooms tighten up, about 4 minutes. Place the mushrooms on a plate.

In the same large skillet over a low simmer, place the whipping cream and Zucchini and Cashew Crème Sauce while continuing to whisk to combine. Let the sauce thicken for a minute or two.

When the pasta is done, drain it and separate any orecchiette that are stuck together. Toss the mushrooms and pasta back into the large skillet with the sauce and heat until warm.

Portion into 2 servings and garnish with the Parmigiano-Reggiano, breadcrumbs, and fresh basil.

TIPS

Watch the breadcrumbs closely, you don't want them to blacken.

You can substitute any kind of mushroom that happens to be in season—I love using chanterelles in this recipe.

Starting Your Own Canning Club

The first week of the month used to feel weighted by bills, worries about everyday tasks, and to-do lists—leaving few thoughts about the future and more regrets about paying for the past. For the last few years, however, the first Wednesday of every month has instead brought anticipation and excitement. Our organizer Brooke Weeber (also this book's illustrator) couldn't have imagined the feelings her canning club would inspire when she reached out to a small group of friends to see if we wanted to meet up and exchange canned goods. Over time, the Portland Preservation Society has grown into much more than the canned food exchange she initiated—it is a reminder for all of us to spread creativity, joy, and delicious food.

Our meeting spot always changes, which brings with it an extra element of surprise. In the summer, we meet in members' backyards and on their front porches, taking advantage of the small window to hold outdoor events. In the winter, we get more creative, descending upon offered living rooms, favorite restaurants, and other local businesses. We see each other's gardens grow and have spent time in one another's kitchens where the goodies are canned. We assemble where the action happens and gaze upon beautiful jars and shelves packed with cookbooks and canning books, passed down from generation to generation.

When you plant a garden, you don't know what it will yield, and that is the same kind of anticipation that builds in me in the days and weeks leading up to our canning meetings. The food exchanging aspect of the group takes a bit of the pressure off each of us; no need to worry about canning every single thing you will miss in the wintertime because other members have likely done some of it for you. There is no way to know who will attend or what they will bring, but the natural ebb and flow of people and ingredients is part of the fun.

As each of our guests walks in, they pull their items out of their bags and place them on the table. Sometimes the jars are beautifully decorated with twine and encyclopedia pages, while others come unlabeled or with vague descriptions scribbled on the metal lid. I personally like to decorate my jars simply with origami paper over the lid that identifies what's inside. Getting my jars ready feels like packing up a piece of myself and giving it to someone special. It is a familiar feeling, akin to knowing you brought just the right birthday present for the guest of honor.

Each time our group meets, we plant seeds for one another by passing on knowledge, ideas, and inspiration. With all the creativity in the group, there is never the worry that everyone will bring the same strawberry jam because it happens to be June. Instead, June's canning club will see strawberry rhubarb shrub, strawberry cognac salt, and strawberry jalapeño jam. There is no judgment or snobbery. Rather, our creations and hard work are all celebrated because of our shared passion and understanding of the efforts made by each and every member. We know there are sometimes mistakes that will be made—we have all experienced an unset jam or a faded pickle—but we want everyone to keep canning. We offer suggestions for future successes and share stories of past failures.

Our gatherings are not exclusive to the canning exchange; we also can together. Working as a collective is fun and also makes a sometimes tedious process go more quickly. At the end of one particular tomato season, we gathered in my backyard to can 200 pounds of tomatoes! We had been planning for months—sourcing from the right farm, getting the gear, picking the date, and finally we were ready. It had been beautiful weather and we planned for a day canning outside on the propane stove. However, as we began washing our tomatoes, it got windy and cold and a full-on storm moved in. So, we did what any Oregonian would do: We set up my farmers' market tent, zipped up our jackets, put our heads down, and got the job done. After the rather soggy work, we enjoyed a nice warm feast inside the house. Perhaps it goes without saying, but out of this group of preservation passionates, great friendships have blossomed.

There is nothing like working hard together to can hundreds of pounds of heirloom tomatoes to create a sense of solidarity and community.

We began as a group of strangers. We preserved food together, picked apples, and shared meals. We each put our own stories, personal histories, and love for canning into the jars we brought to share each month. Over the years, strangers became friends and our friendships have deepened. We keep each other's pantries stocked, but now we also attend each other's art openings, birthday parties, baby showers, and weddings. Through our friendship, we strive to inspire others and keep the tradition of canning alive.

I get a thrill out of hosting the canning club. I hosted our first meeting, and continue to hold the first summer meeting of the year to celebrate our club's anniversary. Every year, it is my task to plan a really great celebration that shows this community how much it means to me. I hope that these stories of our own canning community light the spark that leads to you creating your own group, based on the values of joy, love, and sharing.

Establishing Canning Club Ground Rules

Our group is open to the public so anyone can join and attend, but you can decide if you would rather have yours be made up of new friends or old, though I do highly suggest an open forum as a way to meet new people in your community. I am so thankful for the lifelong friendships I have made with people I may never have met otherwise. We use a social media site to post meeting information and communicate with each other, which works well for our members. The platform is a nice way to create an open discussion about what we have canned or post about other food-related events we want to attend in between our meetings. I suggest you keep your group small, intimate, and fun. We have about twenty active members. If your group gets too big, encourage people to start their own clubs.

Our club meets at a different location once a month, but you and your fellow canners can decide what makes the most sense for you. It is also fun to go to parks, shops, and restaurants. However, if you choose this route, make sure to let the establishment know you are coming so they are ready for you. Call ahead and make arrangements. Meetings usually run about two to three hours. Your group can also meet at U-Pick farms before canning club starts and pick fruit together. Work hard and reward yourselves with the club exchange and a planned picnic.

Another important step in the planning process is determining the number of jars each member should bring to a meeting.

We opted for five jars per person per meeting to keep it manageable. The host starts us off by selecting one jar they would like to keep, and we take turns from there, moving around the circle. There are other canning club formats with trading cards or exchange slips, but we find our method to be simple and effective, and I love that it takes very little organization before each meeting.

It is also a good idea to lay down some ground rules at the beginning so everyone is on the same page. As new members join, these rules can be reviewed. We have found that the following rules stand the test of time and reflect our values.

Use safe practices when canning. Follow guidelines and recipes that come from trusted sources. If you think something you made is unsafe, follow the old mantra: When in doubt, dump it out. Don't risk your health and safety or the health and safety of others.

Items brought to trade must be canned. A canning club is different from a food swap. This rule does have some wiggle room, as sometimes things go in the refrigerator. If this is the case, the jars must be clearly marked.

Canning club is for sharing canned goods you are proud of. Bring items you want to show off, not items that didn't work or that taste bad. You want everyone to leave happy about what they're going home with.

Be respectful and supportive of one another. This includes bringing drinks and snacks to share with the group, helping to clean up when the meeting is over, and offering encouragement to new members.

Create a Shared Feast

Our meetings are always held during the week around dinnertime, and make sure no one leaves hungry. We want the food table to be bountiful, so we ask that all club members bring a dish or snack to share with the group, perhaps even something to go with the item they are trading, such as biscuits with the jam they made. Many of the recipes in this book, from the galette to the tart, were born out of the tradition of making something with the creation I canned and then brought to share with the group. This feast is created by everyone and is for everyone, and there is no pressure put on the host to spend an excessive amount of time or money. Instead, we all pitch in to create an impressive spread featuring our own canning creations.

If you are hosting, set up a food station where your guests can put out the food they have brought to share as they arrive. As a host, I like to build a beautiful cheese and pickle board with fresh cheeses, nuts, herbs, and fruit. I generally cover the table with a tablecloth and pick some flowers from the garden to enhance the environment. I use our ceramic dishes and cloth napkins for less waste (and my husband is really good at doing dishes). Designate somewhere close to the food table to place the dirty dishes and food scraps.

You will also want to include a beverage station. We ask club members to bring some drinks to share and they come with everything from jars of kombucha to jugs of wine to growlers of beer. Keeping with our theme, I put out half-pint canning jars for the glasses. It is important to have something for everyone, which means making sure to offer both alcoholic and nonalcoholic beverages, clearly marked. Along with water, it is nice to serve a nonalcoholic party drink, such as Vanilla Bean Lemonade (page 56). I also like to put out "spa water" (sparkling water with cucumbers and basil). And I always love an excuse to break out my grandma's glass punch bowl. Here is my favorite alcoholic party punch recipe:

Recipe

Makes ten 8-ounce servings

title: PARTY PUNCH

directions:

1 bottle (750 ml) dry, sparkling wine, 2 cups fresh grapefruit juice,

2 cups Vanilla Bean Lemonade, ½ cup elderflower liqueur, 1 teaspoon Cherry Stone Bitters,

1 grapefruit, sliced, for garnish, 3 lavender sprigs, for garnish

Mix all the ingredients in a large punch bowl and garnish with the sliced grapefruit and lavender sprigs. Serve over ice.

Setting Up a Trading Table

The trading table is where the magic happens and it is the heart of the canning swap. The guests do the real work, but here are a few tips to keep in mind. Make sure the table you choose is a sturdy one—no wobbling tables; you don't want to be the cause of a canning club disaster. The trading table is usually the most photographed, so it's nice to place a solid-color tablecloth on the table to make a clean backdrop.

Each of the guests places their five canned items on the trading table as they arrive. If you are hosting, try placing your jars in the middle of the table so guests can carefully add their masterpieces to the mix, building out from your starting point. This way if there are only a few guests, the table won't be lopsided. The location of the table is important: It needs to be away from the food and drinks so it doesn't get bumped and so that people have a chance to eye their first choices. As the event goes on, we naturally migrate from the food and drink tables to the canning table to check out all the beautiful goodies.

What people bring to the trading table changes according to the season. Our summer meeting is bountiful and participation is high. In the cold drizzle of winter, Portlanders tend to hibernate and few people come, but those who do tend to get creative with alcohol infusions, salts, and lots of pressure-canned meats. Although I love a lively summer meeting, it is also a nice change to enjoy a small meeting. One of our members hosted one of my favorite canning club meetings during Christmas. She made a big pot of chicken noodle soup, played holiday records, and we exchanged items around her beautifully decorated tree.

Setting the Mood

You should host canning meetings as you would host a party. Make sure to greet each person who comes in. When new members come to their first meeting, make them feel welcome. If chatting with strangers is not your strong suit, ask someone in the group to be the official new-member greeter. Everyone has made something and the common talking point is canning, so that is a great place to start.

If the overall mood is stark and somber, the meeting will be too. Music can help create a fun, lively vibe. You can set up a music station so guests can select songs, which can also be a fun conversation starter. You can also request a music savvy club member be in charge of making a monthly canning playlist.

Starting the Trading

After everyone has had a chance to put out their canned goods and have a drink and a bite, we call for everyone to gather in a circle around the trading table. Members are welcomed and thanked for coming. Starting with the host, each of us says who we are, what we made, and the best way to eat our item. This is a great opportunity to learn new members' names and listen for the items that sound the most appealing to you. After we have introduced ourselves and our creations, the host gets first choice and we go around in a circle until all the items on the table are gone. As we start taking turns, it often grows quiet while we wonder if the jars we are eyeing will go home with another person. It's kind of like a white elephant gift exchange, except all the prizes are really great!

Awarding Creative Work

I have always loved a rewards system. I believe that when people do hard work they should be honored and celebrated. Having a prize for creating something everyone wants keeps people motivated and it adds a fun vibe to the gathering. In this spirit, the first person to have all five of their jars chosen from the trading table wins a prize. I have loved every prize I have received, but my favorite prize was a unicorn pin, and I continually think about the baby doll head salt and pepper shakers I once almost went home with. Our group is full of creative people, so the prizes have ranged from illustrations, ceramics, and hot sauces, to plants and even fresh garden vegetables. The promise of a prize adds a nice extra treat and a bit of a competitive edge.

Finally, be open to learning as you go and seeing what works for you and your group. Make some traditions, share your stories, and, most of all, have some fun. I'm sure you'll look forward to your canning club meetings every month, just as I do. Keep canning, loving, and sharing within your community!

Stocking Your Pantry

You can't make everything on your own—sometimes you have to leave it to the experts! These items are some of my favorites and are what I like to use for my recipes. This is not a sponsored list, just items I recommend using and want to share with you. Businesses listed have either online ordering or nationwide distribution. Many of the businesses are based in Portland, but I encourage you to seek out other resources that are local to your area.

BAKING

Bob's Red Mill
Stone-milled whole grains, non-GMO flours, oats, polenta, and masa harina
www.bobsredmill.com

King Arthur Flour
The all-purpose flour kings!
www.kingarthurflour.com

Lonesome Whistle Farm
Organic oats, grains, and beans from Junction City, Oregon
www.lonesome-whistle.myshopify.com

The New York Baker
Fresh yeast and professional-grade flour *www.nybakers.com*

BARWARE

Bull in China
For all of your Portland-made fine barware needs
www.bullinchinapdx.com

CANNING, JARS, AND SUPPLIES

Cole Parmer Scientific Experts
pH reader and pH testing supplies: Oakton EcoTestr pH2 Waterproof pocket pH tester
www.coleparmer.com

Food52
Jars, pots, and handmade tools
www.food52.com/shop

Mountain Feed and Farm Supply
California based supply company: Ferment'n Mason Jar Fermentation Kit, Ball Real Fruit Instant Pectin, jelly bag, canning pot, and Kilner stainless jam pot
www.mountainfeed.com

Portland Homestead
Portland-based supply company for urban homesteaders
www.portlandhomestead.com

CHEESE

Beechers Handmade Cheese
Artisan cheese makers in Seattle
www.beechershandmadecheese.com

Point Reyes Farmstead Cheese Company
California-based cheese company
www.pointreyescheese.com

Portland Creamery
Single-origin goat's milk cheese from Molalla, Oregon
www.portlandcreamery.com

COFFEE

Sterling Coffee Roasters
Complex, deep, rich, locally roasted espresso
www.sterling.coffee.com

Water Avenue Coffee
Single-origin coffee, locally roasted: El Toro Espresso Blend, the inspiration for Coffee Braised Onion Jam
www.wateravanuecoffe.com

CUPBOARD

Bee Local Honey
Hot honey and smoked honey made in Portland
www.beelocal.com

Buon Italia
Imported Italian food, including Calabrese crushed red pepper flakes
www.buonitalia.com

Eden Foods
Pure and purifying foods, like tamari and ume plum vinegar
www.edenfoods.com

Glory Bee
Natural products, including tamarind and blue agave
www.glorybee.com

Jacobsen Sea Salt
Kosher and large flake salt, harvested from the Oregon coast
www.jacobsensalt.com

Mountain Rose Herbs
Herbs, spices, dried flowers, gentian root, quassia, citric acid, and cherry bark
www.mountainroseherbs.com

My Spice Sage
Herbs and spices such as annatto powder, smoked paprika, piment d'Espelette, Chinese Five-Spice Powder, asafoetida, coconut oil, and tamarind paste
www.myspicesage.com

Nielsen Massey
Pure vanilla extract, pure almond extract, orange blossom water, and rose water
www.nielsenmassey.com

Old Blue Raw Honey
Raw honey from hives in Oregon, recommended Coriander Honey
www.oldbluenaturalresources.com

Oregon Olive Mill at Red Ridge Farms
Oregon's only commercial olive oil mill, recommended Arbequina Extra Virgin Olive Oil
www.redridgefarms.com

Starvation Alley Cranberry Farm
Organic, unsweetened, cold-press cranberry juice from Washington State
www.starvationalley.com

Whole Foods
Nationwide natural food market with specialty items, such as Canneloni Rustichella D'Abruzzo, hominy, and muscat grapes
www.wholefoodsmarket.com

GARDENING

Uprising Seeds
Organic seeds for your garden
www.uprisingorganics.com

JAM

Plum Tree Jam
Local, pectin-free fruit jams from Oregon
www.plumtreejam.com

Three Little Figs Jam
Small-batch, savory, gourmet jams
www.threelittlefigsjam.com

KITCHEN SUPPLIES

Knotweld
Wood and metalwork company based in the Pacific Northwest, specializing in rolling pins and cutting boards
www.knotweld.com

Michelle Lesniak
Tavern apron dress
www.michellelesniak.com

The Meadow
A beautiful boutique offering salt, salt blocks, chocolate, and bitters.
www.themeadow.com

Webstaurant
Kitchen supplies including aluminum pizza screen and fine-mesh strainer.
www.webstaurantstore.com

Williams-Sonoma
Professional-quality, All-Clad pots and pans, baking slip mat (silicon), baking sheet, All-Clad immersion blender, and Vitamix professional series blender
www.williams-sonoma.com

LIQUOR CABINET

Breakside Brewery
Pacific Northwest Craft Beer: Breakside IPA
www.breakside.com

Dogwood Distilling
The perfect Oregon-made vodka and gin, for infusing
www.dogwooddistilling.com

New Deal Distilling
Portland-based distillers making Ginger Liqueur and Single-Barrel Bourbon Whiskey
www.newdealdistillery.com

MEAT

Olympia Provisions
Charcuterie and gourmet meats
www.olympiaprovisions.com

TABLETOP

KVLCollection
Handmade ceramic plates, bowls, and cups
www.kativonlehman.com

Nell and Mary
Portland-based textile design studio with nice kitchen towels and napkins
www.nellandmary.com

TEA

Mizuba Tea Company
Japanese authentic matcha green tea powder
www.mizubatea.com

Steven Smith Teamaker
Fine teas and herbal infusions: Bergamot Tea
www.smithtea.com

WINE

Union Wine Company
Craft wines from Oregon, including our collaboration spicy wine, Red Haute Pinot, King's Ridge Riesling, and Underwood Rosé, recommended for these recipes
www.unionwinecompany.com

CONVERSION CHARTS

DRY MEASUREMENTS

US	OUNCES	METRIC
½ teaspoon		2 mg
3 teaspoons	½ ounce	15 grams
1 teaspoon	1⁄6 ounce	5 mg
½ tablespoon	¼ ounce	7 grams
1 tablespoon	½ ounce	15 grams
2 tablespoons	1 ounce	30 grams

FLUID MEASUREMENTS

US	PINT	IMPERIAL
¼ cup	–	2 fluid ounces
½ cup	¼ pint	4 fluid ounces
1 cup	½ pint	8 fluid ounces
2 cups	1 pint	16 fluid ounces
4 cups	2 pints (1 quart)	32 fluid ounces

OVEN TEMPERATURES

GAS MARK	FAHRENHEIT	CELSIUS
¼	225º	110º
½	250º	130º
1	275º	140º
2	300º	150º
3	325º	170º
4	350º	180º
5	375º	190º
6	400º	200º
7	425º	220º
8	450º	230º
9	475º	240º

LENGTHS

US	METRIC
⅛ in.	3 mm
¼ in.	6 mm
½ in.	1.25 cm
1 in.	2.5 cm
1 ft.	30 cm

Acknowledgments

It took my entire community of friends and family to make this book happen. I needed all my people to come together for advice, encouragement, recipe testing, editing, and especially tasting these recipes together. Thank you to everyone I know who helped to make this dream come true!

There were many people that had a pre-belief before this book was even a reality: Dirk Marshall believes in all of my ideas from the start and makes sure I go with my crazy thoughts and try new recipes—you started as my band dancer and transitioned to my canning cheerleader. To my proposal editing pals: Tina Boscha, Erin Parker, Mary Crowe, Tara Paluck, and Neha Petal—you ladies really helped work this out from the ground up; you brought structure where there was none. To my super power agent, Deborah Ritchken, thank you for knowing I had something unique and standing by me through it all. To my food friend community, who supported my mission with pre-book quotes and lots of high-fives: Ben Jacobsen (Jacobsen Salt), Union Wine Team, Jami Curl (Quin Candy), Gregory Gourdet, Renee Erickson, and Megan and John (Joy of Cooking). To Ken Norris, for scaring me into paying attention to the compost bucket. Thanks to my ladies Kim Reede, Beverly Adams, and Sarah Masoni—it is inspiring to be around such a wonderful group of gals.

While canning and cooking come natural, the process of creating a book was new to me—and I needed much guidance. To my editor Jordana Tusman, thank you for quickly answering all my questions and guiding this book into a readable state, with gentle encouragement. To my second editor Lynne Ciccaglione, thank you for jumping on board and making things happen. To the dynamic visual team, Caleb Plowman, Natasha Meyers, Rob Perry, Ashley Marti, Jacob Brenner—thank you! To the lay-down stylist queen Kristin Lane, thank you for doing what you do best—you have always been there for me and I love you! To my talented pal Brooke Weeber, for starting Portland Preservation Society, and sharing your illustration talent to enhance this book. You are such a wonderful artist! Thank you for reading and editing, Miranda Rake, Camille Stoch, and Megan Scott, I needed that! To Jarret and Mona (Tournant) for letting me use your lovely home.

None of this could have happened without my farmer friends. Thank you to the farmers who grow our wonderful produce; these recipes would not have happened without you: Rick Steffen and Logan Umbarger (Rick Steffen Farms), Rick Reddaway (Abundant Field Farm), Matthew Garrison (Groundwork Organics), the DeNoble Family (DeNoble Farms), and Art Poulous (La Terra Vita)! Thank you to my recipe testing team, Lindsay Pyrch, Pat Finn, Devery Marshall, Jen Neumann, and especially Anna Galik for testing every single canning recipe! The Portland Farmers Market for providing a gathering place, ingredient access, and my favorite community members that have inspired each and every recipe in this book.

To the Chesa, Parker-Ovelmen, Roadhouse, and Watkins families for reminding me it is important to play, laugh, and eat, especially when things get busy! To my family: Mom, Emmett, Dave, Devery, John, and Ryan—your support and love has made me who I am and I needed you all more during this process than any other! Your love and encouragement brings tears to my eyes. Finally to my daughter, who inspires me to show her how to be a strong woman who can do anything she dreams—you have made my heart full.

My final words are those of encouragement: Food is Love, Give Love.

I have a unique position of being involved in both the social service and the food and farming community. Both are equally wonderful and necessary. Here are some organizations focusing on not only saving and preserving food, but also feeding, inspiring, and helping others! Help comes in many forms, through volunteering, giving money, or word of mouth for some lesser-known agencies. Check out what's in your area, and if there isn't anything like it, start something up!

Local Food Organizations:
Urban Gleaners
Oregon Food Bank
Portland Kitchen
Portland Fruit Tree Project
Culinary Breeding Network
Apples to Applesauce

Local Social Organizations:
Brave Space
Oregon Coalition Against Domestic Violence and Sexual Assault
Portland Women's Crisis Line
Janus Youth Programs
Bradley Angle House

Index

NOTE: PAGE NUMBERS IN *ITALICS* INDICATE FIGURES; PAGE NUMBERS ENDING IN "T" INDICATE TABLES.

D

E

F

O

P

R

S